The Music of Miles Davis

BY LEX GIEL

ISBN 0-634-01040-9

7777 W. Bluemound Rd. P.O.Box 13819 Milwaukee, WI 53213

Copyright © 2004 by HAL LEONARD CORPORATION
International Copyright Secured   All Rights Reserved

For all works contained herein:
Unauthorized copying, arranging, adapting, recording or public performance is an infringement of copyright.
Infringers are liable under the law.

Visit Hal Leonard Online at
www.halleonard.com

CONTENTS

INTRODUCTION 6

PART I: MILES DAVIS: THE COMPOSER
THE ANALYSIS SHEET 9
Analysis sheet notation 10
KEYS AND TONALITIES 12
CHORDS
Basic chords 15
Upper partials 16
Alterations 16
Quartal and quintal chords 17
CHORD FUNCTIONS
Full diatonic 18
Partial diatonic 18
Chromatic 18
Split functions 19
Secondary dominants 19
Diminished 7th chords 20
Diminished 7th chords that function as 7♭9 chords 21
Common usage of diminished 7th chords 23
Augmented chords 23
Common usage of augmented chords 23
SUBSTITUTION
Diatonic substitution 24
Minor 3rd substitution 25
Tritone substitution 26
MODULATION
Internal modulation 27
Unresolved modulation 27
Parallel minor 28
Relative minor 28
Interchange 29
Phrygian major 29
Cycle 30
METHODS OF MODULATION
Prepared modulation 35
Unprepared modulation 36
SONG FORMS
The blues 37
Post points 38
Tags 39
SHOW TUNES
The show-tune melody 40
"My Funny Valentine" (Original Version) 41
Show-tune chords 45
THE JAZZ STANDARD
"My Funny Valentine": The Jazz Changes 49
"My Funny Valentine" (Jazz Changes) 50

PART II: THE COMPOSITIONS

- LITTLE WILLIE LEAPS 56
- BUDO 62
- BOPLICITY (Be Bop Lives) 66
- DIG 72
- THE SERPENT'S TOOTH 76
- TUNE UP 80
- FOUR 86
- SWING SPRING 92
- BLUES BY FIVE 95
- MILES AHEAD 98
- MILES 104
- NARDIS 108
- SO WHAT 113
- FREDDIE FREELOADER 116
- FLAMENCO SKETCHES 118
- PFRANCING (No Blues) 124
- SEVEN STEPS TO HEAVEN 128
- E.S.P. 132
- EIGHTY ONE 140
- STUFF 146
- IT'S ABOUT THAT TIME 149
- MILES RUNS THE VOODOO DOWN 153

PART III: MILES DAVIS: THE PLAYER

SCALES

- Basic scale formulas 156
- Scale analysis 157
- The scales for a minor key 165
- Modes 166
- The blues and pentatonic scales 167

ARPEGGIOS

- Inversions 172
- Advanced arpeggios 172
- Diatonic extensions 173
- Superimpositions 174
- Devices in arpeggios 175

MELODIC DEVICES

- Anticipation 176
- Neighbor tone 176
- Passing tone 177
- Appoggiatura 178
- Auxilary tone 179
- Upper partial 180
- Alterations 180
- Tone behavior 181

PART IV: THE SOLOS

- SIPPIN' AT BELLS 182
- MOVE 188
- DIG 194
- TUNE UP (from *Blue Haze*) 200
- FOUR 204
- SOLAR 208
- VIERD BLUES 214
- MY FUNNY VALENTINE (from *Cookin'*) 218
- TUNE UP (from *Cookin'*) 224
- SID'S AHEAD 232
- MILES 240
- SO WHAT (from *Kind of Blue*) 244
- BLUE IN GREEN 248
- ALL BLUES 253
- SO WHAT (from *At Carnegie Hall*) 260
- MY FUNNY VALENTINE (from *The Complete Concert 1964*) .268
- STELLA BY STARLIGHT 278
- IRIS 288
- CIRCLE 296
- PETITS MACHINS 304
- SPANISH KEY 309

SELECTED DISCOGRAPHY 314

INTRODUCTION

The legacy of Miles Davis is an unprecedented journey of music, creativity, innovation, and personal charisma. His legendary career spanned nearly five decades and he left an indelible impression on the way we think about jazz and the jazz trumpet. Miles was responsible for or contributed heavily to five major movements in jazz from the 1940s to the 1970s: bebop, cool jazz, hard bop, hot jazz, and fusion. In the midst of any type of music he chose to play was his unique, immediately identifiable voice on the trumpet. Every note Miles played wove a tapestry of colors over the music around him in a way that only he could.

In the following pages, the music of Miles Davis is explored in a simple and clear way so that every musician can gain some insight into his genius. PART I studies Miles Davis the composer and explores his abilities and growth as a jazz songwriter. Part II analyzes Miles Davis the player by reviewing his solos and understanding his approach to the jazz solo. In both PART I and PART II the music is presented chronologically to appreciate not only Miles' development, but the progression of jazz as an art form.

In order to organize and clarify the analysis throughout the book, PART I begins with definitions and examples of the music theory relevant to jazz composition, and PART II similarly discusses the theory needed to understand the jazz solo. All of the music theory used is either derived from jazz theory commonly used or adapted classical theory, as jazz has some of its influences from the classical idiom. None of the theoretical tools were created specially for the analysis of Miles Davis and can be used to understand other players in jazz. It should be noted though, that after the evolution of jazz through the 1960s, we have been able to retrospectively create a theoretical language to discuss jazz in a more clear and simple fashion. If you have the opportunity to read biographies of jazz players, especially that go back to the 1940s, you find a mix of knowledge gained through trial and error and knowledge gained from classical theory. As such, many of the devices used were discovered by playing them and not through an organized theoretical system. For example, the widely used ♭5 in the bebop era was simply described as the use of a blue note or half step. It is important to understand this aspect of jazz theory because there are still many jazz education books that subscribe to early methods of jazz soloing and scale usage that don't even begin to explain the language of jazz in the 1950s and beyond. So, if there are theoretical names or devices that you see in the beginning of PART I or PART II that you are not familiar with, take an opportunity to review them as they will help you understand the analysis of Miles' usage of these principles.

PART I
Miles Davis: The Composer

In 1944 a young Miles Davis of eighteen moved to New York City to pursue a career in music. He enrolled in the prestigious Juilliard School of Music with financial support from his father. But, Miles' real incentive to be in New York was to be part of the new jazz being played: bebop. Before long, Miles formed friendships with the two biggest names in bebop, Charlie Parker and Dizzy Gillespie. Parker and Gillespie had been instrumental in reshaping the style of jazz being played. Small groups (trios, quartets, and quintets) would replace the popular big band format. The bebop music used fast tempos, favored swing eighth notes and triplets, and added several new elements to the jazz solo. Their use of alterations and chromaticism would become a trademark for the style.

Miles' studies of classical music at Juilliard soon became cumbersome, as he was learning more from the jazz players on the scene than he was at school. Most of the jazz players in that day learned from each other, since jazz was too new to be taught in the colleges. It wouldn't be until Miles' sextet of the late '50s, that more jazz players would pursue or complete a degree in classical music (for example John Coltrane, Cannonball Adderly, and Bill Evans). Until then, the music was being taught on the street. Dizzy Gillespie's house was the usual gathering place during the day for the bebop players. There the discussions of music were as important to Miles' musical growth as were the nights listening to Charlie Parker in the jazz clubs. During this time, upon Dizzy Gillespie's advice, Miles began to learn piano to better understand the use of chords, a skill that would not be wasted in the years to come.

The bebop songs by and large were a blues, an altered show tune, or based on a show tune. Many of the bebop originals took chords directly from a show tune and used a new melody over the top ("How High the Moon" became "Ornithology," "Honeysuckle Rose" became "Scrapple from the Apple," "Anthropology" was based on "I Got Rhythm," and many others). The bebop melodies usually had complicated themes, more or less like a solo, or sometimes they used simple riffs (repetitive phrases in the melody).

Within a year of Miles' arrival in New York, he was already playing alongside Charlie Parker. His firsthand knowledge of Parker's playing, and guidance from Dizzy Gillespie, certainly showed up in Miles' songwriting style. Miles' contribution to the bebop songbook included: "Donna Lee," "Little Willie Leaps," "Half Nelson," "Sippin' at Bells," and "Milestones" (not the same as the 1958 song of the same name.) "Little Willie Leaps" was recorded in August of 1947 and included Charlie Parker (alto sax), John Lewis (piano), Nelson Boyd (bass), and Max Roach (drums).

In order to understand the most basic and fundamental aspects of a song or solo, a general analysis of the chord progression is presented. This analysis gives us a consistent starting point to work with before discussing more advanced principles. For example, if part of a song is in F Major, we would expect the soloist to use an F Major scale over those chords. This avoids any long, over-detailed explanations of a song or solo and lets us examine techniques we wouldn't immediately expect, such as using F Lydian in the previous example instead of F Major. This basic harmonic analysis is supplied on an analysis sheet that accompanies every lead sheet or solo. This harmonic analysis is provided separately on the analysis sheet so as not to clutter the lead sheet and leave it clear for you to play through.

Example 1: "Solar" – The lead sheet.

SOLAR

By Miles Davis

Copyright © 1963 Prestige Music
Copyright Renewed
International Copyright Secured   All Rights Reserved

THE ANALYSIS SHEET

The analysis sheet examines five fundamental aspects of the chords from the lead sheet:

1. Each **chord** from the lead sheet is written bar-by-bar on the analysis sheet in its basic four-part form.
2. Roman numerals under each chord identify the **chord function** in relation to a key or tonality.
3. A basic **scale** that can be played over the chord is listed under the Roman numerals.
4. The **main key or tonality** is listed at the top of the analysis sheet.
5. The **form** of each song (when applicable) is also listed at the top of the analysis sheet.

Example 2: "Solar" – Basic analysis sheet.

SOLAR

KEY: C Minor
FORM: Minor Blues

Cm(maj7)		Gm7	C7
I		II	V
C HM		F Major	

Fmaj7		Fm7	Bb7
I		II	V
		Eb Major	

Ebmaj7	Ebm7 Ab7	Dbmaj7	Dm7b5 G7b9
I	II V	I	II V
	Db Major		C HM

ANALYSIS SHEET NOTATION

Each chord has its function listed with a Roman numeral referencing the scale degree of its key.

Example 3:

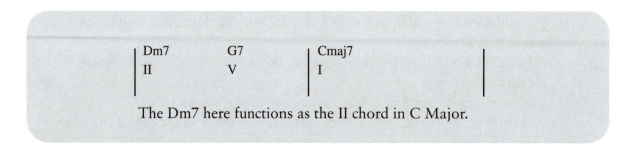

The Dm7 here functions as the II chord in C Major.

Example 4: Below are the basic four-part chords and functions for each scale degree in C Major.

C Major Scale	Basic Chord	Chord Function
C	Cmaj7	I
D	Dm7	II
E	Em7	III
F *subdominant*	Fmaj7	IV
G *dominant*	G7	V
A	Am7	VI
B	Bm7♭5	VII

There are <u>fourteen basic scales</u> that are used in the analysis sheets. Their usage and function will be discussed in Part II, but the scales will be included in Part I for you to come back to later. Below are the fourteen basic scales and any abbreviations that are used:

1. Major
2. Lydian
3. Mixolydian (Mix)
4. Mixolydian ♯4 (Mix♯4)
5. Mixolydian ♭2(♭6) (Mix♭2(♭6))
6. Natural Minor (NM)
7. Harmonic Minor (HM)
8. Tonic Minor (TM)
9. Dorian
10. Phrygian
11. Aeolian
12. Whole Tone
13. Diminished
14. Locrian

Most songs have one main key center. This key, or "tonality," which is used to describe modes, is written at the top of each analysis sheet. When several chords are bracketed on the analysis sheet, it means a new key or tonality has been established which is different from the main key. The Roman numerals and scales under the bracket apply to that new key center.

Example 5: "Tune Up" – The brackets in bars 5-8 show a key change to C Major and in bars 9-12 a key change to B♭ Major. Both key changes have Roman numerals and scales that relate to that key.

TUNE UP

KEY: D
FORM: 16 Bars

Modln.

| Em7 | A7 | Dmaj7 | (Dmaj7) |
| II | V | I | |

Dm7	G7	Cmaj7	(Cmaj7)
II	V	I	
C Major			

Cm7	F7	B♭maj7	Gm7
II	V	I	VI
B♭ Major			

| Em7 | A7 | Dmaj7 | (Dmaj7) |
| II | V | I | |

KEYS AND TONALITIES

Keys or tonalities (which describe the use of modes) are established through chord progressions. Knowing this, it is important to realize that the bass and piano (or accompanying instrument) are most prominently used in establishing the key in a jazz song. As songs and solos are discussed, be careful not to confuse key or tonality names with scale names as they function differently.

Example 6:

Dm7	G7	Cmaj7
II	V	I
C Major		C Lydian ♯4 ♭5 ♯11

In example 6, the chords clearly establish the key of C Major, however the soloist decides to use a C Lydian scale (♯4) over the I chord. The soloist's use of C Lydian will not shift the overall tonality to C Lydian; instead it introduces the color tone of a ♯4 or ♯11 over the Cmaj7 chord.

Similarly, a mode is established as a tonality through the use of chords derived from the mode. Using the previous chord progression in C Major, this time the soloist plays a D Dorian scale (which has the same notes as C Major). Again, the soloist *will not* establish a D Dorian tonality.

Example 7:

Dm7	G7	Cmaj7
II	V	I
D Dorian		

The D Dorian simply sounds out as a C Major scale. So, to play a progression in a mode, one has to be careful not to imply another tonality, especially the major key.

In order to establish the tonality of a mode, we'll examine a few basic methods.

Example 8: Each mode has a characteristic note which sets it apart from the others. This note either best describes the mode or is unique to the mode.

Mode	Characteristic Note	Reason
Ionian	Root	(same notes as major)
Dorian	6th degree	(only minor mode with a ♮6)*
Phrygian	2nd degree	(only minor mode with a ♭2)*
Lydian	4th degree	(only mode with a ♯4)
Mixolydian	7th degree	(only major mode with a ♭7)
Aeolian	3rd degree	(same notes as natural minor)
Locrian	5th degree	(only mode with a ♭5)

Minor mode refers to those modes that contain a ♭3 and a perfect 5th.

Knowing the characteristic note of each mode, we can identify the chords that best establish the mode. The primary chords are the I chord and the two other triads containing the characteristic scale step, counting the diminished triad as primary only in locrian. For example, in D Dorian, B is the characteristic note. The triads in D Dorian that carry the B note are: E Minor (II), G (IV). An effective way to comp in a modal song is to alternate between the I chord and the two chords that carry the characteristic note.

Here is a list of modes with the I chord and the characteristic chords:

Mode	Primary Chords
Ionian	I, IV, VI
Dorian	I, II, IV
Phrygian	I, II, VII
Lydian	I, II, VII
Mixolydian	I, V, VII
Aeolian	I, III, VI
Locrian	I, III, V

Example 9: "So What" uses a set progression of Em11 (II) to Dm11 (I) to establish D Dorian.

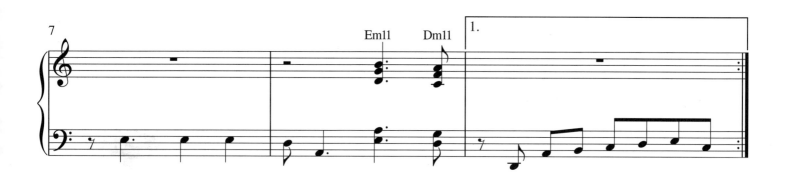

Modal songs frequently list only one chord at the beginning of the song. The single chord indicates that there is no predetermined progression within the mode.

Example 10: "Miles Runs the Voodoo Down" indicates only an F7 chord, using an F Mixolydian tonality. As you can hear on the recording, this has in no way limited the piano players to playing only an F7 chord throughout the song. The pianists play freely using the chords of the mixolydian mode.

CHORDS

BASIC CHORDS

Each chord on the lead sheet has been transferred to the analysis sheet in its basic four-part form.

Basic four-part chords.

Major	Minor	Dim	Aug
maj7	m(maj7)	dim7	+7
7	m7	m7♭5	
	m6		
	m7♭5		

The analysis sheet uses only basic four-part chords because the upper partials and alterations provide color but do not affect the chord function.

UPPER PARTIALS

An upper partial is considered the natural extension of a chord using the major 9th, perfect 11th, or major 13th. For example, extending a B♭maj7 chord to B♭maj13.

ALTERATIONS

An alteration is the sharping or flatting of a chord tone or upper partial. The alterations are: ♭5, ♯5, ♭9, ♯9, ♯11, or ♭13.
(♭5 = ♯4/♭5)

Here is a list of most commonly used upper partials and alterations over the chords in a major and minor key:

Common-chord upper partials and alterations in a major key:

Imaj7:	6, 9, 13 ♭5, ♯5, ♯9, ♯11 (♭9 rare)	**IVmaj7:**	6, 9, 13 ♭5, ♯5, ♯11
IIm7:	9, 11, 13 ♭5, ♯5	**V7:**	9, 11, 13 ♭5, ♯5, ♭9, ♯9, ♯11, ♭13
IIIm7:	9, 11, (13 rare) ♭5, ♯5	**VIm7:**	9, 11, 13 ♭5, ♯5
		VIIm7♭5:	11 ♭13

Common-chord upper partials and alterations in a minor key:

Im7:	9, 11, 13 ♭5, ♯5	**IVm7:**	9, 11, 13 ♭5, ♯5
IIm7♭5:	11 ♭13	**V7:**	11 ♭5, ♯5, ♭9, ♯9, ♯11, ♭13
IIImaj7:	9, 13 ♭5, ♯5, ♯11	**VImaj7:**	9, 13 ♭5, ♯5, ♯11
		VIIdim7:	no common upper partials or alterations

QUARTAL AND QUINTAL CHORDS

Quartal and quintal chords are commonly used in comping, especially in modal songs. Quartal chords are created by stacking perfect or augmented fourths or both.

Example 11: In D Dorian, a quartal chord can be created from each note in the scale.

Similarly, a quintal chord is created by stacking diminished or perfect fifths or both.

Example 12: Quintal chords in D Dorian.

Because the chord is voiced in repetitive fourths or fifths, the identity of the chord is ambiguous. These chords are not creating the tension of the V chord nor the resolution of the I chord. Instead, the quartal or quintal chord creates both power and the feeling of suspension, resisting the active and passive functions. Quartal and quintal chords express the overall tonality and not a specific function within the mode. The accompanist therefore can use all seven quartal and quintal chords interchangeably. This gives the song a feeling of chord movement without the basic chord ever changing.

CHORD FUNCTIONS

FULL DIATONIC

Full diatonic means the chord is part of the main key.

Example 13: In F Major the full-diatonic chords are:

F Major	Chord Function
Fmaj7	I
Gm7	II
Am7	III
B♭maj7	IV
C7	V
Dm7	VI
Em7♭5	VII

PARTIAL DIATONIC

Partial-diatonic chords have roots that are part of the key but their spelling or species is not.

For example, in the key of F Major, Dm7 is the full-diatonic VI chord. A VI used as a secondary dominant chord (see page 19) changes the species to a 7th (D7). The root of the chord (D) is diatonic to F Major (part of that key), but the species has changed from Dm7 to D7, making D7 partial diatonic.

CHROMATIC

Chromatic chords have roots that are not diatonic to the key.

A common jazz blues progression is:

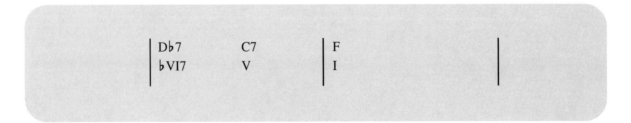

The ♭VI7 is an example of a chromatic chord. Its root (D♭) is not in the key of F Major. However, its function is still related to the key of F Major, distinguishing a chromatic chord from a modulation (a chord progression which establishes a new key).

SPLIT FUNCTIONS

Getting in and out of new keys and cycles is often achieved by using a chord that has an identity in both keys.

Example 14: "Blue in Green" – The Dm7 in bar 3 acts as the I chord in D Minor *and* the III chord in B♭ Major. The B♭maj7 in bar 5 acts as both the I in B♭ Major and the VI in D Minor. The Dm7 in bar 10 acts as the IV in A Minor and the I in D Minor.

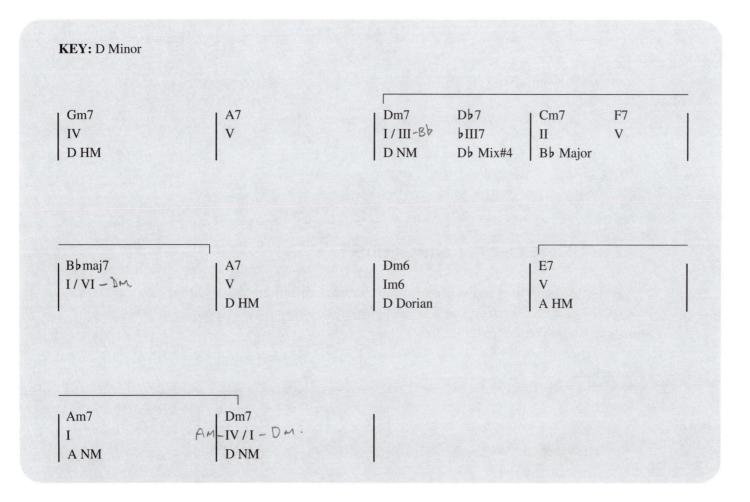

SECONDARY DOMINANTS

A secondary-dominant chord is a 7th chord used to create the impression of a V to I resolution. The chord assuming the role of the I chord will always be full diatonic to the key. The secondary dominant is partial diatonic to the key.

Secondary dominants in a major key:

Secondary dominant	of	Diatonic chord
I7		IV
II7		V
III7		VI
VI7		II
VII7		III

Example 15: "Little Willie Leaps" – First 4 bars – Dm7 is used in bar 3 as a VI7 chord or a secondary dominant to the II chord (Gm7) in bar 4.

KEY: F Major

Fmaj7	Gm7 C7	Am7 D7	Gm7 C7
I	II V	III VI7	II V
		D Mix♭2(♭6)	

Secondary dominants in a minor key:

Secondary dominant	of	Diatonic chord
I7		IV
II7		V
III7		VI

DIMINISHED 7TH CHORDS

A diminished 7th chord is made up of all minor 3rd intervals. A Gdim7, for example, is G B♭ D♭ F♭. Since the chord is made up of all minor 3rd intervals, any chord tone can act as a root.

Example 16:

G dim	=	G	B♭	D♭	F♭
B♭dim7	=	B♭	D♭	F♭	A♭♭(G)
D♭7	=	D♭	F♭	A♭♭(G)	C♭♭(B♭)
Edim7 (F♭dim7)	=	E	G	B♭	D♭

Note: Enharmonic notes are used to simplify the chord names or spellings or both.

DIMINISHED CHORDS THAT FUNCTION AS 7♭9 CHORDS

There is a strong relationship between diminished 7th chords and 7th chords. Because of this, some lead sheets use a diminished 7th chord in place of a 7th chord.

A diminished 7th chord can be converted into a 7♭9 chord with four identities. Take the Gdim7 of the previous example, lower its root a half step and name that a 7♭9 chord (G♭7♭9).

Example 17:

Gdim7	=	G♭7♭9
G	=	(A♭♭) the ♭9th of G♭7
B♭	=	the 3rd of G♭7
D♭	=	the 5th of G♭7
F♭	=	the 7th of G♭7

Now, using the minor 3rd intervals of the diminished 7th chord, there are also three other chords that are spelled with the same notes as G♭7♭9:

Example 18:

		♭9th	3rd	5th	7th
G♭7♭9	=	A♭♭(G)	B♭	D♭	F♭
A7♭9	=	B♭	C♯(D♭)	E(F♭)	G
C7♭9	=	D♭	E(F♭)	G	B♭
E♭7♭9	=	F♭	G	B♭	D♭

Even though dim7 and 7th chords are interchangeable in spelling, their function differs greatly. The most common confusion is notating a chord as a diminished 7th when it is functioning as a secondary dominant.

Example 19:

| Am7   Ebdim7 | Gm7   C7 |
| III   VI | II   V |

By lowering the Ebdim7 a half step and deriving its 7th chord names, you can determine if any act as a secondary dominant to the following chord:

Ebdim7   =   D7b9   F7b9   Ab7b9   Cb7b9

The D7b9 is the secondary dominant of Gm7 and should be notated as such:

Example 20:

| Am7   D7b9 | Gm7   C7 |
| III   VI7 | II   V |

Two common reasons why the dim7 notation is used in place of the 7b9 chord notation:

1. The root of the diminished 7th chord helps to control the bass note for voice leading.

Example 21: The (E) in Am7 moves to the (Eb) in Ebdim7 to the (D) in Gm7.

| Am7   Ebdim7 | Gm7   C7 |
| III   (VI7) | II   V |

2. The second problem with notating a 7th chord as diminished 7th chord, is that the 7th chord takes Mix, Mix#4, or Mixb2(b6) as a scale solution. The diminished chord, however, takes a diminished scale.

COMMON USAGE OF DIMINISHED 7TH CHORDS

Below are examples of diminished 7th chords functioning as diminished 7th chords. These are the most common progressions:

Example 22:

I	Idim7	II
I or III	♭IIIdim7	II
IV	♯IVdim7	V or I/ with the 5th in the bass
V	Vdim7	V
II	♯IIdim7	III

AUGMENTED CHORDS

The augmented chord is a triad consisting of all major 3rd intervals. Its primary scale is the whole tone scale. The augmented triad can be extended to an augmented 7th chord (+7) since the ♭7th is included in the whole tone scale. The notation of the +7 and 7♯5 are often used interchangeable in jazz notation. However, the +7 functions as an extension of an augmented triad, whereas the 7♯5 is a 7th chord with an altered 5th.

COMMON USAGE OF AUGMENTED CHORDS

The following progressions show common uses of augmented chords.

I	I+	I6 or IV		
I	I+	I6	I7	IV
IV	IV+	V		
V	V+	V		
VI	♭VI+	I/ with the 5th in the bass		

SUBSTITUTION

DIATONIC SUBSTITUTION

In a major key, the V chord stands out from the other full diatonic chords because it carries a tritone between the 3rd and the 7th. The V chord is considered an *active* chord because of the tension the tritone creates. Active basically means the chord needs to be resolved due to its tension. The note most characteristic of the V chord is the 7th. Since the 7th of a V chord distinguishes the chord as active, then the other chords containing that note can be considered active as well.

Example 23: Chords containing the 7th of the V chord or the 4th degree of the key.

In C Major:		**Active chords**
II	-	Dm7
IV	-	Fmaj7
V	-	G7
VII	-	Bm7♭5

When the tritone in the V chord resolves to the I chord, the 7th of the V resolves to the 3rd of the I, and the 3rd of the V resolves to the root of the I.

Example 24: Note resolution of a V → I in C Major.

V7 chord		**I chord** (as a triad)
G	→	G
B	→	C
D	→	C
F	→	E

Example 24 is typical of a V to I resolution in classical music. The pull of the 7th degree of the key (B) to the root (C), and the pull of the 4th degree of the key (F) to the 3rd (E), are the primary examples of tone behavior. Tone behavior, simply put, is the natural tendency of one note to move to another note. This concept will be very important as Miles' soloing style is explored, and will be examined in greater depth in PART II.

Since the 3rd of the I chord resolves the 7th of the V chord, the I chord is considered a *passive* or resolutional chord. So, any chord containing the third of the key is also *passive* and therefore resolutional.

Example 25:   In C Major: Passive chords
  I   -   Cmaj7
  III   -   Em7
  VI   -   Am7

Diatonic (or direct) substitution is therefore the substitution of any *active* chord for another *active* chord, and any *passive* chord for another *passive* chord.

MINOR 3RD SUBSTITUTION

Minor 3rd substitution principle – 7th chords are interchangeable with each other if their roots are minor thirds apart.

Example 26:

C7 can be replaced with: E♭7   G♭7   B♭♭7(A7)

This works because the notes of the three minor 3rd substitutes are useable chord tones, upper partials, or alterations over C7 (see page 16).

Example 27:

E♭7   *Note function over C7*   A7   *Note function over C7*
E♭ = ♯9(D♯)   A   = 13th
G   = 5th   C♯ = ♭9th(D♭)
B♭ = 7th   E   = 3rd
D♭ = ♭9th   G   = 5th

G♭7   *Note function over C7*
G♭ = ♭5th
B♭ = 7th
D♭ = ♭9th
F♭ = 3rd(E)

If C7 were the V chord in F Major, then the chord function for the three minor 3rd substitutes would be: E♭7 = ♭VII7, G♭7 = ♭II7, A7 = III7.

Example 28: "Swing Spring" – The bridge repeatedly uses the ♭II7 in place of the V.

B♭m7	A7	A♭m7	G7
II	♭II7	II	♭II7
A♭ Major	A♭ Mix♯4	G♭ Major	G Mix♯4

Gm7	G♭7	Fm7	F7
II	♭II7	V	V
F Major	G♭ Mix♯4	E♭ Major	(B♭ Major)

Note: A ♭II7 chord is usually used to connect the II and I chords. This creates a chromatic line between the roots of all three chords (example: Gm7 to G♭7 to Fmaj7).

TRITONE SUBSTITUTION

The tritone substitution is included in the minor 3rd substitution principle. Extending the C7 chord out to E♭7, then G♭7, the distance between C and G♭ is an augmented 4th or tritone. Tritone substitution is identified apart from minor 3rd substitution, because the tritone is situated precisely at the middle of a key. In the middle of a key, the tritone has equal pull between the root and the octave, suspending the tonality and resisting tension or resolution. The most common use of the tritone substitution is the ♭II7, connecting the II to the I chord. The ♭II7 is the tritone substitute for the V chord.

MODULATION

INTERNAL MODULATION

A new key is established and resolves to the I, VI or III chord (listed in order of resolutional strength). The new key is shown on the analysis sheet with brackets over the top to distinguish it from the main key and other modulations.

Example 29: Bars 1 and 2 show chords in the main key of C Major, while bars 3 and 4 show a modulation to B♭ Major with a bracket over both bars.

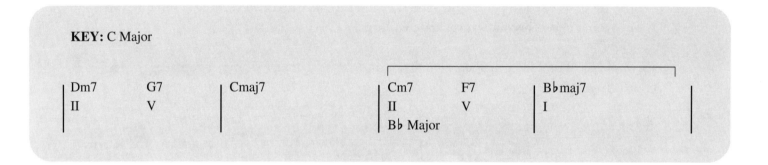

UNRESOLVED MODULATION

A new key is entered, but does not use the resolutional I, VI, or III chord. The chords are bracketed together and any chord or chord function under the bracket will be part of the new key, the same as an internal modulation.

Example 30:

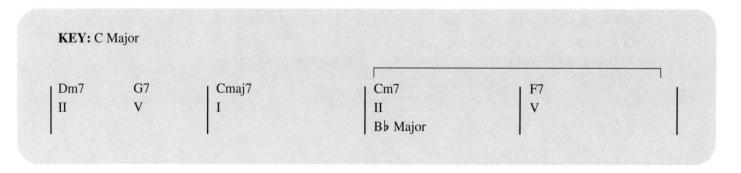

PARALLEL MINOR

Parallel Minor is the minor key with the same root as the major key. Example: E♭ Major's parallel minor is E♭ Minor. This relationship is used in several ways:

1. The song modulates from a major key to its parallel minor (or vice versa).

2. The **tonic interchange:** ending a series of chords in a major key on the I(maj7) chord and then playing the Im7.

3. The **Tierce de Picardie** or **Picardy Third.** This technique uses the parallel major tonic chord in place of the minor tonic chord. Simply put, in a minor key the Imaj7 is used in place of the Im7. Using the picardy third technique, the major tonic chord becomes a surprise ending.

Example 31: The Tierce de Picardie – In a minor key the Imaj7 (B♭maj7) replaces the Im7 chord (B♭m7).

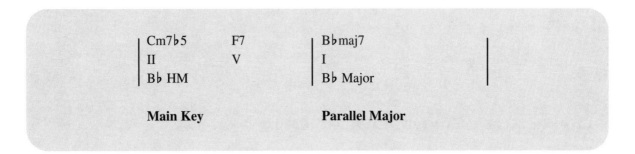

RELATIVE MINOR

The relative minor is the minor key whose key signature is the same as a major key. Its root is the 6th degree of the major scale. For example, A is the 6th degree of C Major and A Minor has the same notes as C Major. Frequently, songs move back and forth between the major and relative minor because of this relationship. For example, A is the 6th degree of C Major, and A Minor has the same notes as C Major.

INTERCHANGE

When playing in a minor key, you may notice that certain chords are not full diatonic minor, but are borrowed from a parallel mode (a mode with the same root). This concept originated in classical music. Many classical composers treated the chords of natural minor, harmonic minor, and melodic (tonic) minor as interchangeable. All three scales contain a minor triad as a I chord. With this in mind, they could always move in and out of the three, knowing the resolutional I chord would be the same. Extending this concept further, many jazz songs borrow from the parallel modes as well. For example, a song in C Minor may borrow chords from C Dorian, C Phrygian, or C Aeolian. The borrowed chords are analyzed as partial diatonic to the main key, since the new key or mode is not firmly established.

PHRYGIAN MAJOR

This is a colorful device used in flamenco music. Basically, the soloist is playing a phrygian scale, while the accompanist plays a major triad of the I chord. For example, a soloist can play in E Phrygian (E F G A B C D) while the accompanist plays an Emaj triad (E G♯ B). The phrygian major scale is then the phrygian scale with a major 3rd (E F G♯ A B C D). There is no clash between the phrygian scale (E F G A B C D) and the major chord (E G♯ B), because the G♮ note acts as a blue note (♭3rd or ♯9th). Common progressions include Imaj–II or Imaj–II–III–II.

Example 32: "Flamenco Sketches" – In bars 13 through 20 of the song, Bill Evans plays in D Phrygian Major while Miles solos in D Phrygian.

CYCLE

A cycle is a group of chords related to each other by either equidistant interval, equidistant root interval, or identical species.

Intervallic cycle – The chords in this cycle are equidistant in root interval and share the same species. The most common intervallic cycles are ascending perfect 4th (asc. P4), and ascending or descending minor 2nd (asc. minor 2nd or desc. minor 2nd).

Example 33: One of the most common cycles is an ascending perfect 4th cycle. This is typically referred to as the "I Got Rhythm" changes, based on chord changes to "I Got Rhythm" by George Gershwin. The strength of this particular asc. P4 cycle is all of the chords are partial or full diatonic to the key.

KEY: A♭ Major

cycle asc. P4

C7	F7	B♭7	E♭7
(III7)	(VI7)	(II7)	(V)

The distance from C to F is an interval of a perfect 4th, as is the case between F and B♭; B♭ and E♭. The chords in a cycle may have a relationship to the main key, but are still identified as a unit because of their unique symmetric relationship.

Root cycle – In this cycle only the roots of the chords are equidistant by a common interval. The chord species are not the same.

Example 34: "Circle" – First 16 bars – Root cycle bars 11 through 13.

KEY: D Minor

Dm7		Dm6	Bbmaj7
I		Im6	VI / I
D NM		D Dorian	D NM

Ebmaj7	D7	Bm7	Cmaj7
IV	V	III	IV
Eb Lydian	G Major		

root cycle asc. minor 3rd

(Cmaj7)		Gmaj7	Abmaj7
		I /	
			Ab Major

A7	Fmaj7	A7	(A7)
/ V	III	V	
D HM	D NM	D HM	

Species Cycle – This cycle is based on identical chord species. No intervallic relationship of roots is necessary.

Example 35: Species cycle in bars 5 and 6.

KEY: F

| Fmaj7 | | Gm7 | C7 |
| I | | II | V |

species cycle

Dmaj7	Bmaj7	Gmaj7	Emaj7	Fmaj7		Gm7	C7
				I		II	V
D Lydian	B Major	G Lydian	E Major				

METHODS OF MODULATION

Internal modulation is the change from one key to another key within a section or song. The internal modulation is a harmonic module within the main key. The relationship between the key of the modulation and the previous key (either the main key or another internal modulation), is based on how closely related the two keys are to each other. This relationship of keys can be broken down into three main categories:

1. The I chord of the modulation is **full diatonic** to the previous key.

    The key of C Major modulates to another key whose I chord is full diatonic to C Major.

    Dm7 the II chord in C Major becomes the I chord in D Minor.
    Em7 the III chord in C Major becomes the I chord in E Minor.
    Fmaj7 the IV chord in C Major becomes the I chord in F Major.
    Am7 the VI chord in C Major becomes the I chord in A Minor.

Example 36: "Boplicity" – First 8 bars – In bars 4 and 5, the song modulates from the main key of F Major to the key of B♭ Major. The B♭maj7 in bar 5 is the I chord of the new key (B♭ Major) while being full diatonic in the previous key (F Major).

Gm7	Fmaj7	Gm7	C7	Fmaj7	Cm7	F7
II	I	II	V	I	II	V
					B♭ Major	

B♭maj7	Gm7	C7	Fmaj7
I / IV	II	V	I

2. The I chord of the modulation is **partial diatonic** to the previous key.

The key of C Major modulates to another key whose I chord is partial diatonic to C Major.

C Major modulates to D Major, Dmaj7 is partial diatonic to C Major.
C Major modulates to E Major, Emaj7 is partial diatonic to C Major.
C Major modulates to F Minor, Fm7 is partial diatonic to C Major.
C Major modulates to G Major, Gmaj7 is partial diatonic to C Major.
C Major modulates to A Major, Amaj7 is partial diatonic to C Major.
C Major modulates to B Major, Bmaj7 is partial diatonic to C Major.

Example 37: "Seven Steps to Heaven" – Bars 13 through 20 – F Major modulates to C Major, or to the key of the dominant (V chord). This modulation is particularly common in classical music.

G7			E♭maj7	Emaj7	Fmaj7	
II7			♭VIImaj7	VIImaj7	I	
G Mix			E♭ Lydian	E Major		

Cmaj7	Dm7	G7	Em7		Fm7	B♭7
I	II	V	III		II	V
C Major						

3. The I chord of the modulation is **chromatic** to the previous key.

This is a less common type of modulation because the new key has little in common with the previous key. In the previous examples of *full* and *partial diatonic* modulations, you will notice the difference between the previous key and the key of the modulation is only separated by one accidental. "Boplicity" modulated from the key of F Major (1 flat - B♭) to the key of B♭ Major (2 flats - B♭ and E♭). Similarly, "Seven Steps to Heaven" modulated from F Major (1 flat - B♭) to the key of C Major (no sharps, no flats). In a *chromatic* modulation the key centers will usually be much farther apart.

Example 38: "Budo" – Bars 21 through 28 – This is a typical chromatic modulation in jazz songs. The root of the implied I chord in each modulation in bars 21, 22, and 23 are chromatic to the previous key. The difference in each key is much greater than the previous examples: bar 21 C♭ Major (7 flats), bar 22 B♭ Major (2 flats), bar 23 A Major (3 sharps), bar 24 A♭ Major (4 flats). The strength of this modulation instead lies in the fact that each key is a minor 2nd interval away from the previous key. The symmetrical movement lessens the oddity of the modulations acting much like a cycle.

D♭m7	G♭7	Cm7	F7	Bm7	E7	B♭m7	E♭7
II	V	II	V	II	V	II	V
C♭ Major		B♭ Major		A Major		(A♭ Major)	

| A♭maj7 | | | | B♭m7 | | E♭7 | |
| I | | | | II | | V | |

PREPARED MODULATION

A *prepared modulation* is when the chord used to begin the modulation is *active* in the new key.

Entering and exiting a modulation can be carefully planned where the move from one key to another is a smooth transition. A common way to enter or exit a modulation is with the use of a pivot chord. In entering a modulation, a pivot chord has an identity in the previous key and in the key of the modulation. Similarly, when exiting a modulation, a pivot chord has an identity in the key of the modulation and in the key following the modulation. This pivot chord is usually full diatonic to the modulation, and is either full diatonic, partial diatonic, or chromatic to the key before or after the modulation.

1. A **full-diatonic pivot chord** is a pivot chord with a full-diatonic function in the key before or after the modulation and in the key of the modulation.

Example 39: "Seven Steps to Heaven" – Bars 1 through 4 – The Em7♭5 in bar 2 is the full-diatonic VII chord of the main key (F Major) and the full-diatonic II chord of the new key (D Minor). Similarly, the Dm7 in bar 3 is the full-diatonic I chord of D Minor and the full-diatonic VI chord in F Major. This is also a good example of a modulation to the key of the relative minor.

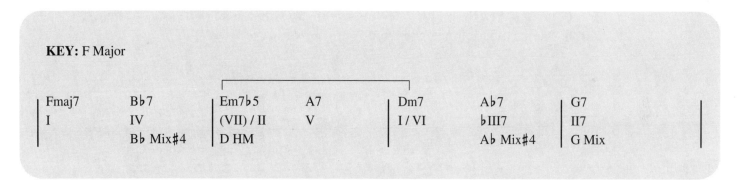

Similarly, when exiting a modulation, a pivot chord has an identity in the key of the modulation and in the key following the modulation.

2. A **partial-diatonic pivot chord** is partial diatonic to the key before or after the modulation.

One of the most common ways to establish a new key using a partial-diatonic pivot is with the use of an interchange.

Example 40: "Four" – Bars 1 through 4 – The E♭m7 in bar 3 acts as an interchange for the E♭maj7 in bars 1 and 2, meaning the roots stay constant while the species change.

KEY: E♭ Major

E♭maj7		E♭m7	A♭7
I		II	V
		D♭ Major	

3. A **Chromatic pivot** is a chord chromatic to the key before or after the modulation.

Example 41: "The Serpent's Tooth" – Bars 1 through 8 – The A♭7 in bar 4 acts as the V in D♭ Major and as the ♭VII7 in the following key of B♭ Major. The ♭VII7 is a chromatic chord in B♭ Major functioning as the minor 3rd substitute for the V (F7).

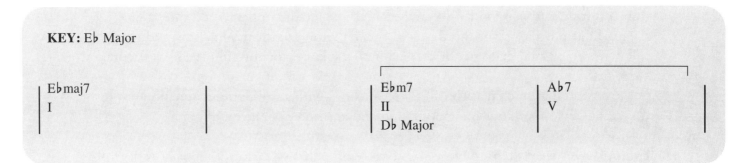

B♭maj7	G7	Cm7	A7	Dm7	D7	E♭m7	A♭7
I	VI7	II	VII7	III	III7	II	V / ♭VII7
	G Mix♭2(♭6)		A Mix♭2(♭6)		G Mix♭2(♭6)	D♭ Major	

B♭maj7	E7	E♭maj7	A♭7	B♭maj7		(B♭maj7)	
I	♭II7	I	IV7 / ♭VII7	I			
	E Mix#4	E♭ Major	A♭ Mix#4				

UNPREPARED MODULATION

An *unprepared modulation* is when the chord used to begin the modulation is *passive* in the new key.

In example 39, "Seven Steps to Heaven," the song resolves in bar 4 to the I chord (Fmaj7) of the main key (F Major) and modulates to the I chord (Cmaj7) in C Major. The Cmaj7 is a *passive chord* in C Major making the modulation unprepared. All pivot chords will function the same in unprepared modulations and prepared modulations.

SONG FORMS

All jazz songs use a basic structure(s) within which themes are developed. Here is a list of some of the most common forms:

12-bar blues (Example: "Blues by Five")
16 bars (Example: "Tune Up")
32 bars: AABA form (Example: "Budo")
    A Section — 8 bars
    Repeat A — 8 bars (sometimes using a different second ending)
    B Section — 8 bars (new chords, new melody)
    Repeat A — 8 bars (using first or second ending)

The AABA form is one of the most widely used forms in jazz with four sections of 8 bars creating a 32-bar head. Other forms include odd-numbered bar lengths such as a 10-bar theme (Example: "Blue in Green") or a 45-bar theme (Example: "Stuff"). Being aware of the basic structure helps you understand the development of themes. The AABA song form or similar structures are marked on the analysis sheets in the top left corner.

THE BLUES

The blues is a fundamental part of jazz writing. The most basic form of a blues is the 12-bar blues.

Example 42: Basic major blues in F.

F7 I F Mix			
B♭7 IV B♭ Mix		F7 I F Mix	
C7 V		F7 I F Mix	

Note: In a major blues the I and IV chords are typically 7th chords (I7 and IV7). Because of this common usage, the analysis sheets will show the chord functions simply as I and IV.

Example 43: Basic minor blues in F Minor.

Fm7 I F NM				
B♭m7 IV		Fm7 I		
C7 V F HM		Fm7 I F NM		

POST POINTS

The post points in a blues are the key chords (I, IV, and V) and their bar and beat location. The post points should be considered indispensable to a 12-bar blues.

Blues post points on beat 1 of indicated bars (major or minor):

> Bar 1   —   I
> Bar 5   —   IV
> Bar 7   —   I
> Bar 9   —   V
> Bar 11 —   I

In a jazz blues, chords are often added or substituted throughout the head. But, in general, you will find the post points remain a constant in each head.

TAGS

A tag is an extended ending to a song. The tag is used in place of the original I chord resolution. Here are three of the most common tags shown in the key of F Major.

Tag 1

G7 / II7 / G Mix	Gm7 / II C7 / V	G7 / II7 / G Mix	Gm7 / II C7 / V
G7 / II7 / G Mix	Gm7 / II C7 / V	Fmaj7 / I	

Tag 2

Am7 / III (or IIIm7♭5)	D7 / VI7 / D Mix♭2(♭6)	Gm7 / II	C7 / V
Fmaj7 / I			

Tag 3

Bm7♭5 / #IVm7♭5 / B Locrian	B♭m6 / IVm6 / B♭ Dorian	Am7 / III	A♭7 / ♭III7 / A♭Mix#4
Gm7 / II	G♭7 / ♭II7 (or ♭IImaj7) / G♭ Mix#4	Fmaj7 / I	

SHOW TUNES

Show tunes were a key influence on jazz song writers. Songs from Rodgers and Hart, Cole Porter, George Gershwin, Oscar Hammerstein, Jerome Kern, and many others became part of the list of songs that were considered jazz standards. The sensibility of the melodies and sophisticated use of chord progressions provided an excellent vehicle for jazz improvisation. The show-tune writers were already using the common II → V → I progression, secondary dominants, chord substitutions, cycles, and modulations. Some writers, such as George Gershwin, were even incorporating elements of the blues into their songs.

Typical elements of a show tune:
- AABA form or some derivative.
- Thematic melodies making use of melodic repetition or rhythmic patterns to create an easily identifiable melody.
- Advanced chord progressions that sometimes use arranging techniques to connect the chords.

THE SHOW-TUNE MELODY

Show tunes typically establish a theme within each section. For example, the first A section of an AABA song is usually 8 bars, and the melody resolves or comes to a close in bar 7 or 8. Most of the show tunes ended a melodic theme on root, third, or fifth of the key providing a resolution to the theme. They also ended a theme on the seventh, providing tension like an active chord to push the song forward to the next section. Tone behavior was also greatly considered in developing a theme. This includes the natural pull of the second (re) to the root (do), the seventh (si) to the octave (do), and the fourth (fa) to the third (mi). Tone behavior was often used in closing a theme. For example, if the A section ended on the root of the key, it was often preceded by the second or the seventh creating a re → do or si → do resolution.

"My Funny Valentine" was a favorite of Miles and a good example of a show tune from Rodgers and Hart. "My Funny Valentine" uses an AABA song form in 8-bar sections with the last A section extended by 4 bars.

Part I | MILES DAVIS: THE COMPOSER

MY FUNNY VALENTINE
from BABES IN ARMS
Original Version

Words by Lorenz Hart
Music by Richard Rodgers

Copyright © 1937 (Renewed) by Chappell & Co.
Rights for the Extended Renewal Term in the U.S. Controlled by Williamson Music and WB
Music Corp. o/b/o The Estate Of Lorenz Hart
International Copyright Secured   All Rights Reserved

Following is an analysis of the melody in "My Funny Valentine." The melody is discussed one section at a time, looking at elements such as melodic construction, rhythmic motifs, and thematic resolution. The melody is viewed only in relation to the main key (C Minor) and not the chords. By doing this, the impact and strength of the melody as it stands alone can be understood. Understanding a show-tune melody apart from the chords is important for several reasons:

1. The melodies were carefully constructed to provide memorable themes that existed independent of the chords.

2. The melodies often would outline or indicate the chords that should be played under it.

3. Knowing the construction and flow of a melody will help you understand how and why jazz players used chord substitutions for a show tune.

Example 44: First A section (A1) of "My Funny Valentine."

Bars 1 and 2 establish the first motif both in terms of melodic phrasing and rhythmic patterns.

Bars 3 and 4 repeat bars 1 and 2.

Bar 5 repeats bar 1.

Bar 6 repeats the rhythm of bar 1. It descends the C Natural Minor scale from B♭ to A♭ to G, preparing for the theme's ending on the 4th (F) in bar 7.

Bars 7 and 8 end the theme on the 4th of C Minor. The 4th provides tension like an active chord to push forward to the next section.

Example 45: Second A section (A2) of "My Funny Valentine."

Bars 9 through 13 are a shift of the melody in A1. The theme begins on the 3rd of C Minor instead of the root, but mirrors the motif melodically and rhythmically otherwise. This device was used in many show tunes to provide variety to the song and yet keep the melody identifiable.

Bar 14 mimics the descending pattern in A1. In A2, however, there is the addition of a chromatic passing tone (CPT). A chromatic passing tone connects two diatonic notes by one-half step. In this case, the A♮ connects the B♭ to the A♭.

Bars 15 and 16 end section A2 on the 6th degree of C Minor (A♭).

Example 46: B section (B) of "My Funny Valentine."

Bars 17 and 18 establish the first motif for the B section.

Bars 19 and 20 are a repeat of bars 1 and 2 with the exception of the C on beat 1 of bar 3.

Bar 21 repeats bar 17, replacing B♭ on beat 1 with D. The D concludes the rise in the melody that began in bar 17 with B♭ (B♭ → C → D).

Bar 22 repeats the rhythm of bar 18, ascending the C Natural Minor scale from E♭ instead of descending.

Bars 23 and 24 end the B section theme, resolving to the root of C Minor (C). The D note in bar 24 prepares for the return of the A section.

Example 47: Third A section (A3) of "My Funny Valentine."

Bars 25 and 26 repeat bars 1 and 2 of A1.

Bars 27 and 28 repeat bars 9 and 10 of A2.

Bars 29 and 30 repeat bars 1 and 2 of A1, one octave up.

Bars 31 and 32 resolve the A3 theme on the 3rd of C Minor (E♭).

Bars 33 and 34 (**extended ending**) repeat bars 9 and 10 of A2.

Bars 35 and 36 again resolve A3 to the 3rd of C Minor (E♭).

As is typical with some show tunes, the third A section is a combination of A1 and A2.

Note: Notice too how the resolutional note of each section spells an Fm7 chord:

section A1 → F   section A2 → A♭   section B → C   section A3 → E♭

SHOW-TUNE CHORDS

Most chords for a show tune directly support the melody (or vice versa). The bulk of the chords use the melody note on a chord change as a chord tone (a root, third, fifth, or seventh of the chord). In "My Funny Valentine," for example, bar 1 begins with a Cm chord on beat 1 and a C in the melody (the root of Cm). The chords in a show tune that don't use this technique were used for one of the following reasons:

- The chord provides contrast to the melody.

- The chord is part of a progression that together provides movement under the melody.

- The chord is part of a specific voice-lead progression (a progression where a note from each chord creates a diatonic or chromatic line).

Rodgers and Hart used all of the previous techniques to create the chord progression for "My Funny Valentine."

Example 48: A1 of "My Funny Valentine."

Bars 1 through 4: the chords are all essentially Cm, which supports the repetitive use of C and E♭ in the melody. There are four different species of Cm used to create a chromatic line from the notes of the chord:

$$
\begin{aligned}
\text{Cm} &\rightarrow \text{C} \\
\text{Cm/B} &\rightarrow \text{B} \\
\text{Cm7} &\rightarrow \text{B♭} \\
\text{Cm6} &\rightarrow \text{A}
\end{aligned}
$$

Bar 5: the A♭ substitutes for Cm as a passive chord. It still complements the C and E♭ in the melody, only this time they are the chord-tone 3rd and 5th of A♭.

Bars 6 through 8 use all active chords, holding out on any resolution until A2. This supports the melody's use of a thematic ending in bars 7 and 8, but not a melodic resolution since it ends on the 4th of C Minor (F).

Example 49: A2 of "My Funny Valentine."

Bars 9 through 12: the chords create the same chromatic line as in A1, with the G7 replacing Cm/B in bar 10. The G7 is used to support the shift up in the melody, which now has an F in bar 10.

Bars 13 and 14 repeat the chords of A1.

Bars 15 and 16 prepare for the B section, as does the melody. Notice how the sustained A♭ in the melody is the root of A♭m in bar 15, and the 7th of B♭7 in bar 16. The A♭m and B♭7 chords begin a modulation to the relative major of C Minor, E♭ Major.

Example 50: B Section of "My Funny Valentine."

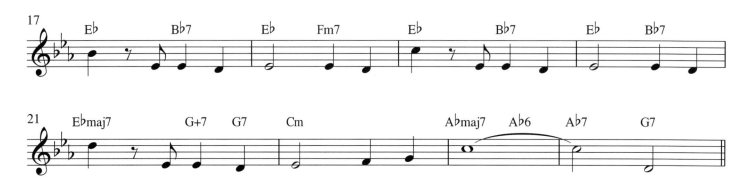

Bars 17 through 20: the melody has a strong use of the note E♭, much as A2 did. In the B section, however, there is movement between passive and active chords in the relative major (E♭ Major).

Bar 21 ends the modulation to E♭ Major and prepares for the return to C Minor on beat 3 using a G7 (the V in C Minor). The G+7 is used simply to support the melody (D♯, the ♯5 of G7, is enharmonically the E♭ note in the melody).

Bars 22 through 24 prepare for the return to the A section. Bar 22 restates bar 9 of A2. The melodic ending on C is supported by the A♭ chord in bar 7. The D melody in bar 24 is supported by G7, which awaits resolution to the I chord in A3.

Example 51: A3 of "My Funny Valentine."

Bars 25 through 29 use the chords from A1 to support the melody that is created from parts of both A1 and A2.

Bars 30 and 31 use the melody as chord tones to deliver a final resolution in C Minor: II7 → V → I.

Bars 32 through 36 melodically retrace A2, while the supporting chords end the song in the relative major (E♭ Major).

Here is a complete analysis of the chords to "My Funny Valentine."

Cm I C NM	Cm/B Im(maj7) C HM	Cm7 I C NM	Cm6 Im6 C Dorian
A♭ IV C NM	Fm7 IV C NM	Fm6　　　G7 IVm6　　V F Dorian　C HM	Fm7　　　G7 IV　　　V
Cm I C NM	G7 V C HM	Cm7 I C NM	Cm6 Im6 C Dorian
A♭ VI C NM	Fm7 IV	A♭m IVm A♭ Dorian	B♭7 V E♭ Major
E♭　　　B♭7 I　　　V	E♭　　　Fm7 I　　　II	E♭　　　B♭7 I　　　V	E♭　　　B♭7 I　　　V
E♭maj7　G+7　G7 I　　　　V 　　　　C HM	Cm I C NM	A♭maj7　A♭6 VI	A♭7　　　G7 VI7　　　V A♭ Mix♯4　C HM
Cm I C NM	Cm/B Im(maj7) C HM	Cm7 I C NM	Cm6 Im6 C Dorian
A♭ VI C NM	D7♭5　　G7 II7　　　V D Mix　　C HM	Cm I C NM	E♭7 I7 E♭ Mix
A♭　　　A♭maj7 IV	Fm7　　　B♭7 II　　　V E♭ Major	E♭ I	(A♭7　　G7) VI7　　　V A♭ Mix♯4　C HM

THE JAZZ STANDARD

As mentioned earlier, songs from the show-tune writers were regularly included in the jazz repertoire. The jazz version of a show tune, however, made several changes to the original song. The melody was often embellished either by the addition of notes to the main melody, or through improvisation over the chords. Both types of changes to the melody were improvised at the players discretion. This is partly why every version of a standard sounds different in jazz, even by the same musician. The chords to a show tune were changes as well. This varied from basic substitution to reharmonization (where the new chords and modulations are added that are radically different from the original). The incentive for jazz players to use different chords was really for the solos and not as much for the head (the beginning of a jazz song where the main melody and chords are stated). For example, a lot of show tunes use only one chord for up to 4 bars. A jazz version adds chords or substitutions to create more movement in the chords and more momentum for the soloist.

"MY FUNNY VALENTINE": THE JAZZ CHANGES

On the following page is the lead sheet for "My Funny Valentine," using a common set of jazz chord changes. These are not the chords Miles used in his versions of the song, as you will see later in the book. They are, however, a set of changes that most jazz musicians use for "My Funny Valentine." Understanding these changes against the originals will help you understand how jazz standards were developed, and eventually understand the chords Miles used.

MY FUNNY VALENTINE
Jazz Changes

KEY: C minor
FORM: AABA

Cm	Cm(maj7)	Cm7	Cm6
I	Im(maj7)	I	Im6
C NM	C HM	C NM	C Dorian

A♭maj7	Fm7	Dm7♭5	G7♭9
IV	IV	II	V
C NM	C NM	C HM	

Cm	Cm(maj7)	Cm7	Cm6
I	Im(maj7)	I	Im6
C NM	C HM	C NM	C Dorian

A♭maj7	Fm6	A♭m6	B♭7
VI	IVm6	IVm6	V
C NM	F Dorian	A♭ Dorian	E♭ Major

E♭maj7	Fm7	Gm7	Fm7	E♭maj7	Fm7	Gm7	Fm7
I	II	III	II	I	II	III	II

E♭maj7	G+7	G7	Cm	B♭m7	E♭7	A♭maj7	Dm7♭5	G7
I	V		I	II	V	I / VI	II	V
	C HM		C NM	A♭ Major			C HM	

Cm	Cm(maj7)	Cm7	Cm6
I	Im(maj7)	I	Im6
C NM	C HM	C NM	C Dorian

A♭maj7	Dm7♭5	G7♭9	Cm	B♭m7	E♭7
VI	II	V	I	II	V
C NM	C HM		C NM	A♭ Major	

A♭maj7	Fm7	B♭7	E♭6	Dm7♭5	G7♭9
I / IV	II	V	I	II	V
	E♭ Major			C HM	

Example 52: A1 of "My Funny Valentine" (jazz changes).

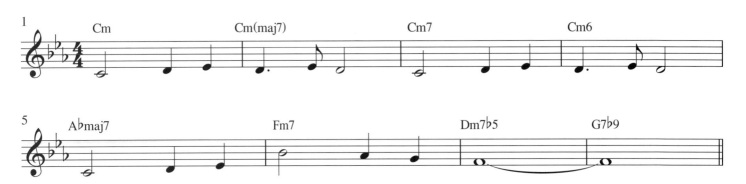

Section A1 follows the original changes with the exception of Dm7♭5 in bar 7 replacing Fm6 and G7. The Dm7♭5 still supports the F note in the melody, while providing the more preferred II → V → I in jazz (root movements in fourths or fifths are stronger and more resolutional).

Example 53: A2 of "My Funny Valentine" (jazz changes).

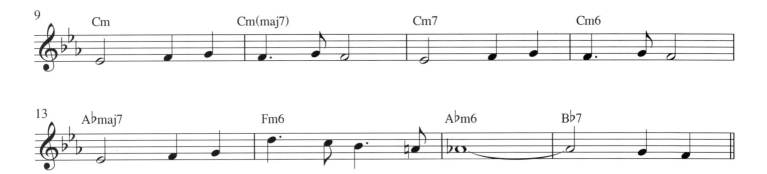

Bars 9 through 13 repeat the chords from A1. The G7 used in bar 2 of the original version is replaced with the Cm(maj7), favoring the use of Cm against the chromatic line.

Bar 14: the Fm6 replaces the original Fm7 to support the D note in the melody.

Bars 15 and 16: the A♭m6 in bar 15 replaces the original A♭m. An A♭m6 is the same spelling as an Fm7 chord, creating more of a II → V in bars 7 and 8.

Example 54: B Section of "My Funny Valentine" (jazz changes).

Bars 17 through 20: each original B♭7 (V) is replaced with its active substitute, Fm7 (II). Similarly, the E♭ (I) in bars 18 and 20 is replaced with its passive substitute, Gm7 (III). By doing this, the chords create more movement by rising and falling twice by scale step.

Bar 21: the G+7 on beat 3 repeats the original chord. However, the ♯5 is not needed in the solo changes and can be replaced with a straight G7.

Bars 22 and 23 add a quick modulation to A♭ Major. The A♭maj7 in bar 23 has a split function between acting as the I chord in A♭ Major and the VI chord in C Minor.

Bar 24 replaces the original A♭7 with a Dm7♭5, again favoring the II → V progression.

Example 55: A3 of "My Funny Valentine" (jazz changes).

Bars 25 through 31 use the original chords, replacing the D7♭5 in bar 30 with a Dm7♭5.

Bars 32 and 33: a B♭m7 is added in bar 32. Any 7th chord can be preceded by its II chord through active for active substitution. In doing this, bar 32 creates another modulation to A♭ Major, where the A♭maj7 is now both the I chord in A♭ Major and the IV chord in the upcoming modulation to E♭ Major.

Bars 34 through 36 repeat the original changes, again replacing the A♭7 with a Dm7♭5.

PART II The Compositions

"LITTLE WILLIE LEAPS"

Miles used the chords from Kaper and Kahn's song "All God's Chillun Got Rhythm" for this song. The entire song is in the key of F Major with two short modulations to A Major, and one to D Major. All three modulations are unresolved where the V chord of each modulation functions as a secondary dominant in F Major.

The melody for "Little Willie Leaps" is essentially a bebop solo. Unlike the repetitive themes of a show tune, a bebop solo usually tries to avoid repetition, making the melodies less memorable. A theme is alluded to in bars 1 and 2, but quickly left to the solo-like structure that follows. Some elements of this melody will be discussed, however a review of PART IV on solos will help you better understand this melody.

LITTLE WILLIE LEAPS

From the recording *The Immortal Charlie Parker, Volume 2* (Charlie Parker)

By Miles Davis

© 1948 (Renewed 1976) SCREEN GEMS-EMI MUSIC INC.
All Rights Reserved   International Copyright Secured   Used by Permission

LITTLE WILLIE LEAPS

KEY: F
FORM: ABAC

Fmaj7			Gm7	C7	Am7	D7♭9	Gm7	C7♭9
I			II	V	III	VI7	II	V
						D Mix♭2(♭6)		

Fmaj7			Gm7	C7	Am7	D7♭9		
I			II	V	III	VI7		
						D Mix♭2(♭6)		

Bm7	E7		Am7	D7	Gm7	C7	F6	
II	V / VII7		III	VI7	II	V	I	
A Major				D Mix♭2(♭6)				

Em7	A7		Dm7	G7	Gm7		C7	
II	V / III7		VI	II7	II		V	
D Major				G Mix				

Fmaj7			Gm7	C7	Am7	D7♭9	Gm7	C7♭9
I			II	V	III	VI7	II	V
						D Mix♭2(♭6)		

Fmaj7			Gm7	C7	Am7	D7♭9		
I			II	V	III	VI7		
						D Mix♭2(♭6)		

Bm7	E7		Am7	D7	Gm7	C7	F6	
II	V / VII7		III	VI7	II	V	I	
A Major				D Mix♭2(♭6)				

Gm7	C7	F6	
II	V	I	

Example 56: Section A from "Little Willie Leaps."

The bebop soloist often began a chord change playing a chord tone, much as the show-tune writers had in their melodies. This stemmed out of the early jazz improvisers like Louis Armstrong, who would use chord tones almost exclusively in their solos. As jazz improvisation progressed, placing the chord tone on the chord change made the solo follow the chords. Yet, *between* the chord changes the use of upper partials, alterations, and chromaticism was heavily exploited in connecting chord tones. As you look through all four sections of "Little Willie Leaps," you will find this to be true on nearly every chord change.

Bar 1: C over Fmaj7
Bar 2: G over Gm7
Bar 3: C over Am7, F♯ over D7♭9
Bar 4: B♭ over Gm7, E over C7♭9
Bar 5: A over Fmaj7
Bar 6: B♭ over Gm7
Bar 7: C over Am7
Bar 8: F♯ over D7♭9

Miles also makes strong use of chromaticism in this melody. Typical to the bebop era was the use of chromatic neighbor tones (CNT). As I discussed tone behavior on page 24, the 7th degree (leading tone) of a key has a natural pull to the octave. The bebop players began using this idea over any chord. The leading tone was used to enter a phrase or arpeggio, usually on the upbeat of four or two, just before the chord change.

Example 57: Chromatic neighbor tone (CNT).

In example 57, the G7 is the V chord in C Major. The F♯ in bar 1 is chromatic to the key. The F♯ quickly introduces the G7 arpeggio, giving it an added push. It is not repeated in the main G7 arpeggio as it violates the seventh (F) of the chord.

As chromaticism progressed in bebop, any chord tone was subject to an introduction from a note a half step above or below it (a chromatic neighbor tone). Miles makes use of this device in bar 4, preceding the E on beat 3 with a D♯. Similarly, in bar 6 Miles uses a C♯ as a chromatic neighbor tone to D. In this case, the C♯ is placed on the upbeat of one, another common placement of a chromatic neighbor tone in bebop other than the upbeat of two or four.

Example 58: Section B of "Little Willie Leaps."

Miles uses a Bdim arpeggio over E7 in bar 9. The B in Bdim is the 5th of E7, the D is the 7th of E7, and the F is the ♭9 of E7. The F note on the upbeat of four also acts as a diatonic neighbor tone to the E in bar 10, resolving down by a half step. Bar 10 uses an A♭ over a D7 chord, the common ♭5 in bebop. In bar 11 Miles uses a chromatic line with chromatic passing tones (CPT) that carefully connects notes to end on F (the root of the key) in bar 12. Bar 15 also makes use of a ♭5 over the Gm7.

Example 59: Section C of "Little Willie Leaps."

Bars 25 through 28 are a repeat of those in the B section. Bars 29 through 32 end the head with a chromatic neighbor tone in bar 29 and another chromatic line in bar 30 that resolves the melody on the root (F).

Another great hangout for musicians developed at Gil Evans' apartment. Gil Evans was a self-taught arranger, whose unique style would contribute to Miles' work on and off over the years. Apart from names like Charlie Parker and Dizzy Gillespie, Evans' apartment included musicians like Gerry Mulligan, John Lewis, Lee Konitz, and George Russell. Talk around the apartment often centered on the idea of forming a group to showcase the arranging talents of some of the players. The combined decision was to create arrangements for a nonet (nine-piece band). This was a small number of instruments compared to a big band, which was the typical vehicle for the arrangers. But, the economy of instruments was considered to be just the right amount to develop the harmonies and still be functional. While Evans, Mulligan, and Lewis worked out the arrangements, it was Miles' drive and focus as a leader that brought the group to life. Miles managed to book the nonet for an engagement at the Royal Roost, a jazz club in New York at the time. This was no small feat considering the club had to pay nine players in contrast to the usual five or less. Undoubtedly, Miles' stature in the jazz community helped, as he had been playing alongside Charlie Parker for a couple of years. The Royal Roost turned out to be the only club dates for the nonet, but Miles managed to secure a record contract with Capitol Records as well. The recording sessions were difficult to organize, and it would take three sessions over more than a year to record the material that became known as The Birth of the Cool.

Cool jazz used a lot of the bebop language, even using fast tempos in some numbers. The feel of the music is what differed so much from bebop. The soloist often had a softer voice and focused on the middle register instead of the upper, a notable preference of Miles throughout his career. Cool jazz made use of more whole, half, and quarter notes, contrasting the flurry of eighths and triplets that dominated bebop.

Miles contributed three songs to The Birth of the Cool sessions: "Budo," "Deception," and "Boplicity."

"BUDO"

"Budo" is a bebop tune that is credited to both Bud Powell and Miles Davis (Bud Powell recorded the tune under the name "Hallucinations"). The song was arranged by John Lewis and included the following players: Miles Davis (trumpet), Kai Winding (trombone), Junior Collins (french horn), Bill Barber (tuba), Lee Konitz (alto sax), Gerry Mulligan (bari sax), Al Haig (piano), Joe Shulman (bass), and Max Roach (drums). The song is an AABA form. A2 is a repeat of A1 with a new ending in bars 7 and 8, and A3 repeats A2.

BUDO

From the recording *Birth of the Cool* (Miles Davis)

By Miles Davis and Bud Powell

BUDO

KEY: A♭
FORM: AABA

A♭maj7		B♭m7	E♭7
I		II	V

D♭	G7♭9	Cm7♭5	F7	B♭m7	E♭7	A♭maj7	E♭7
IV	#VI7	II	V	I / II	V	I	V
D♭ Mix#4	G Mix♭2(♭6)	B♭ HM					

A♭maj7		B♭m7	E♭7
I		II	V

D♭	G7♭9	Cm7♭5	F7	B♭m7	E♭7	A♭maj7
IV	#VI7	II	V	I / II	V	I
D Mix#4	G Mix♭2(♭6)	B♭ HM				

Cm7	F7	B♭maj7
II	V	I
B♭ Major		

D♭m7	G♭7	Cm7	F7	Bm7	E7	B♭m7	E♭7
II	V	II	V	II	V	II	V
C♭ Major		B♭ Major		A Major			

A♭maj7		B♭m7	E♭7
I		II	V

D♭	G7♭9	Cm7♭5	F7	B♭m7	E♭7	A♭maj7
IV	#VI7	II	V	I / II	V	I
D♭ Mix#4	G Mix♭2(♭6)	B♭ HM				

Example 60: A1 and A2 of "Budo."

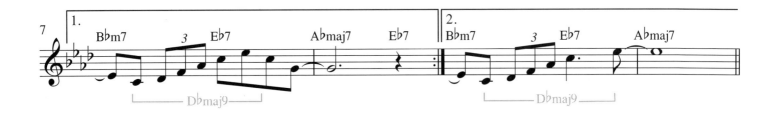

The A section chords are predominantly a II → V → I in A♭ Major. Bar 5 begins with a D♭7, the IV7 of the key, bringing a blues element into the song. Also in bar 5, a modulation to B♭ Minor begins with the ♯VI7 chord. Since the VI chord in B♭ minor is G♭maj7, a ♯VI7 chord (G7) is used to act like a secondary dominant to the II chord (Cm7♭5). The relationship between the two chords in bar 5, is that the G7 is the tritone substitute for D♭7. In bar 7, the B♭m7 is used as a full diatonic pivot, functioning as the I chord in B♭ Minor and the II chord in A♭ Major.

The melody is more thematic than most bebop songs. A chromatic line in bar 2 is followed by a D♭maj7 arpeggio in bar 3. Similarly, a semi-chromatic line in bars 5 and 6 is followed by a D♭maj9 arpeggio. The strength of these lines is that they are constructed of chord tones or alterations of the chords they are played over (see example 60). The D♭maj7 arpeggios are a direct extension of the B♭m7 chord they are played over. Each arpeggio begins with its leading tone, moving by a half step into the D♭ note. The D♭, F, and A♭ are all chord tones of B♭m7 (third, fifth, and seventh) and the C acts as the ninth. The D♭maj9 arpeggio in bar 7 functions the same over B♭m7, moving all the way up to an E♭ note to compliment the E♭7 chord on beat 3. The second ending of the A theme uses the D♭maj9 arpeggio again, this time ending the theme on E♭ (the 5th in A♭ Major) instead of the G note (the 7th in A♭ Major) in section A1.

Example 61: Section B of "Budo."

The B section melody is less thematic, creating more of a bebop solo. Bar 18 uses a chromatic neighbor tone (E♮) to move into the E♭ note and a ♯9 (G♯) on beat 4 over the F7. A chromatic passing tone connects the chord changes in bar 21 and in bar 23.

BOPLICITY
(Be Bop Lives)

From the recording *Birth of the Cool* (Miles Davis)

By Miles Davis and Gil Evans

BOPLICITY

KEY: F
FORM: AABA

Gm7	Fmaj7	Gm7	C7	Fmaj7	Cm7	F7#5
II	I	II	V	I	II	V
					Bb Major	

| Bbmaj7 | | Gm7 | | C7 | | Fmaj7 |
| I / IV | | II | | V | | I |

Gm7	Fmaj7	Gm7	C7	Fmaj7	Cm7	F7#5
II	I	II	V	I	II	V
					Bb Major	

| Bbmaj7 | | Gm7 | | C7 | | Fmaj7 |
| I / IV | | II | | V | | I |

Cm7	F7#5	Cm7	B7	Bbmaj7		
II	V	II	bII7	I		
Bb Major			Bb Mix#4			

Bbm7	Eb7#5	Bbm7	A7	Ab	Abm7	Gm7	C7
II	V	II	bII7	I	bIIIm7	II	V
Ab Major			A Mix#4		Ab Dorian		

Gm7	Fmaj7	Gm7	C7	Fmaj7	Cm7	F7#5
II	I	II	V	I	II	V
					Bb Major	

| Bbmaj7 | | Gm7 | | C7 | | Fmaj7 |
| I / IV | | II | | V | | I |

"Boplicity" was recorded four months after the first session and included some different players in the nonet: Miles Davis (trumpet), J J Johnson (trombone), Sandy Siegelstein (french horn), Bill Barber (tuba), Lee Konitz (alto sax), Gerry Mulligan (bari sax), John Lewis (piano), Nelson Boyd (bass), and Kenny Clarke (drums). The song features an arrangement by Gil Evans and in general delivers more of the cool jazz feel than "Budo." The "Boplicity" melody combines the bebop language with more laid-back rhythms and sustained notes, and it is played at a medium tempo. "Boplicity" is another AABA song form, with the second ending to the A section adding only one note in preparation for the B section.

Example 62: A section of "Boplicity."

The chords for the A section are mostly a II → V → I in F Major. A short modulation to the key of the IV chord is established in bar 4, with the B♭maj7 splitting its function in bar 5. The melody uses a lot of chord tones in the A section to create the theme. As we have seen in "Budo," a D♭maj7 arpeggio was played over a B♭m7 chord. The notes of the D♭maj7 arpeggio functioned over the B♭m7 as beginning on the 3rd of B♭m7 and ending on the 9th. Miles reverses this idea in bars 4 and 5 of "Boplicity," beginning arpeggios on the 9th of the chord and descending to the 3rd. Even bar 6 alludes to this, using the 7th and 9th of Gm7 as melody notes. In bar 7, Miles uses an Fmaj7 arpeggio (the arpeggio of the I chord) over the V chord (C7). This resolves the melody a bar early, while the chord delays resolution until bar 8. The melody in bar 8 sustains a B♮ to end the theme, played over an Fmaj7 chord. The B♮ functions as a ♯11 over the Fmaj7, a popular alteration in jazz over the I chord. This undoubtedly stemmed in part from George Russell's influence at Gil Evans' place. Russell would later author the book *The Lydian Chromatic Concept of Tonal Organization* which emphasized, among other things, the use of the ♯11 (or ♯4 in Lydian) over the I chord. As discussed on page 24, the fourth degree of a major key is responsible for the active chords. The addition of the fourth degree (maj11) to a I chord would add active elements to the highly resolutional chord. This is why the I chord never takes a maj11, instead using the ♯11 which has become a distinctive jazz color tone. A soloist, as well, does not typically sustain the fourth degree, using it only in passing perhaps as part of a scale run. This explains Miles' use of a sustained B♮ at the end of the A theme.

Example 63: Section B of "Boplicity."

Bars 17 through 20 in the B section make another modulation to the key of B♭ Major (the key of the IV chord). Miles uses a B7 in bar 18 (the tritone substitute for the V) as a way to create a descending chromatic line in the arrangement. Bar 17 begins with a D note in the melody, the 9th of Cm7, and proceeds to C♯ over an F7♯5 chord. From there the chord arrangement continues the chromatic line using the root of each chord (C → B → B♭). Bar 21 uses a tonic interchange to enter the key of A♭ Major. Miles then sets up the same chromatic line as before, using the previous chord progression transposed to A♭ Major. In bar 23, a tonic interchange is used again to move back into the main key of F Major.

The melody of the B section is slightly more dense than that of the A section. However, the melody is still highly thematic, unlike the B section for "Budo." The melody in bar 17 begins with a descending arpeggio, again beginning on the ninth, with the C♯'s on beat 2 anticipating the F7♯5. Bar 18 resembles bar 17 down one octave. Bars 19 and 20 move through the B♭ Major scale with the addition of some thirds as the I chord resolves. Bars 21 through 24 reinforce the B theme, as the notes from bars 17 through 20 are transposed to the A♭ Major modulation. There are some changes made to the melody in bars 23 and 24 to accommodate the return to F Major. The use of A and C in bar 24 again allude to the I chord arpeggio played over the active II and V chords.

By the end of 1948, Miles was no longer playing clubs with Charlie Parker, reducing their association to only recording dates. The final nonet was finally completed in March of 1950. While Miles was already well-known in the jazz community, his ability to consistently sell records under his own name was as yet to be proven. In 1951, Prestige signed Miles on to a one-year contract, giving him just such an opportunity. Miles' second recording date for Prestige yielded the album Dig. *Apart from work as a leader, this was Miles' first chance to take advantage of new recording technologies. The 78 rpm records that had forced artists to record songs in under three minutes, was gradually being replaced by 33 1/2 rpm long-playing records. This was an important advancement for the jazz players, whose studio recordings never seemed to capture their abilities as a live performer. Miles took full advantage of the recording opportunity, playing each of the songs for the date over four minutes, with his song "Bluing" lasting nearly ten minutes. Miles contributed four originals to the session ("Dig," "Denial," "Bluing," and "Out of the Blue") with, as usual, an impressive group of players: Miles Davis (trumpet), Sonny Rollins (tenor sax), Jackie McLean (alto sax), Walter Bishop (piano), Tommy Potter (bass), and Art Blakey (drums).*

"DIG"

For the song "Dig," Miles used the chords from "Sweet Georgia Brown." The song uses an ABAC form, with a main key of A♭ Major. The chords of A1 connect with the B section to create a 12-bar cycle, with each chord partial or full diatonic to A♭ Major. Miles adds one modulation to the chords in the last bar of the B section. The original chords to "Sweet Georgia Brown" call for a III7 chord in this bar. In A♭ Major, the main key of "Dig," the III7 chord is C7, which Miles moves to beat 3. Preceding the C7 with its II chord (Gm7), Miles creates a little more momentum getting back to the A section. The short modulation to F Major then splits the function of the F7 in section A2 as the I7 in F Major and the VI7 in the main key, A♭ Major. The cycle that was created from A1 to B is abandoned in section A2 to section C. This leaves the chords to A2 partial diatonic to A♭ Major. The chords of section C round out the song in A♭ Major, making use of secondary dominants in bars 26 and 30.

"Dig" is a bebop tune, and the melody certainly employs typical bebop phrasing. The themes, however, make good use of melodic and rhythmic repetition. The melody for "Dig" shows Miles' ability to create a more memorable melody, which isn't as evident on the other originals of this session.

Example 64: Section A of "Dig."

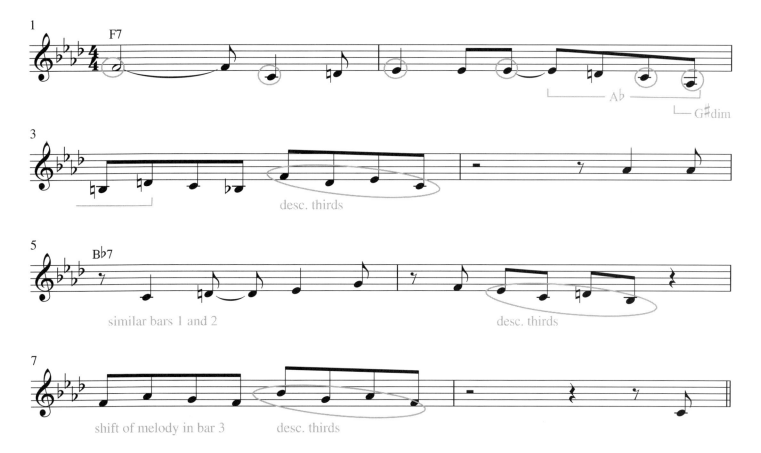

In bar 1 and into bar 2 is the outline of the F7 chord. Rhythmically, Miles begins the theme slow using quarter and half notes. Bars 2 and 3 employ eighth notes and give more of a bebop feel to the melody. Notice the use of two arpeggios over F7: an A♭ arpeggio (A♭ is the ♯9 of F7, C is the 5th, and E♭ the 7th) and a G♯dim arpeggio (G♯ is the ♯9 over F7, B is the ♯11 or ♭5, and D is the 13th) with the A♭ note in the melody being the enharmonic G♯. The statement in bars 1 through 3 is ended with the use of descending thirds, which Miles uses two more times in the A section theme. Bars 5 through 7 are repetitive structures using thematic material from bars 1 through 3 (see example 64).

DIG

From the recording *Dig* (Miles Davis)

By Miles Davis

Copyright © 1964 Davis Family Publishing, Nut Brown Ale Music and Second Floor Music
Copyright Renewed
All Rights on behalf of Davis Family Publishing and Nut Brown Ale Music Administered by
Sony/ATV Music Publishing, 8 Music Square West, Nashville, TN 37203
All Rights outside the U.S. Controlled by Prestige Music
International Copyright Secured All Rights Reserved

DIG

KEY: A♭
FORM: ABAC

F7 (VI7) F Mix				
B♭7 (II7) B♭ Mix	cycle asc. P4			
E♭7 (V) E♭ Mix				

A♭maj7 I	B♭m7 II	E♭7 V	A♭maj7 I	Gm7 II F Major	C7 V

F7 I7 / VI7 F Mix				
B♭7 II7 B♭ Mix				

Fm7 VI	C7 III7 C Mix♭2(♭6)	Fm7 VI		E♭7 V

A♭maj7 I	F7 VI7 F Mix♭2(♭6)	B♭m7 II	E♭7 V	A♭maj7 I

Example 65: Section B of "Dig."

Rhythmically, Miles reverses his approach of the A section in his B section melody. Eighth notes begin the B section theme, ending with longer durations. He uses a #11 twice in this theme, the second time ending the theme much as he did in "Boplicity." The Fm7 arpeggio shows Miles' use of notes that exploit the upper partials of a chord instead of the chord tones (F is the 9th of Eb7, Ab is the 11th, C is the 13th, and Eb is the root). Chord tones create consonance, upper partials provide color, and alterations create tension or color or both. As jazz evolved from bebop to hard bop and hot jazz, the emphasis on chord tones was replaced by the emphasis on upper partials and alterations. Miles' use of both upper partials and alterations (from section A) is not the exception in bebop, but rather shows a general trend that would lead to other styles. Bars 13 through 16 of the B section are a solo section in the head. This was used frequently in bebop songs, where the melody is not predetermined and the soloist(s) improvises through this section of the song.

Example 66: Section C of "Dig."

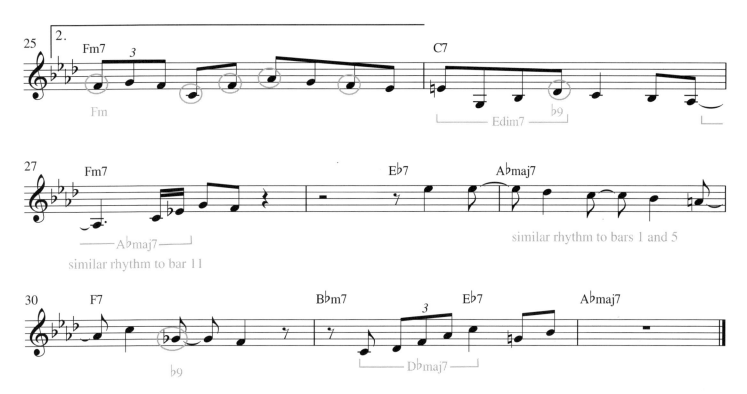

Section C adds some new melodic material, but borrows rhythmic statements from both the A and B section (bar 3 and bars 5 and 6). The three arpeggios Miles uses in bars 26, 27, and 31 all begin on the third of the chord they are played over, and end on the ninth (as Miles had done previously in "Budo" and "Boplicity").

In January of 1953, Miles entered the studio under a new contract from Prestige. He pulled together five noteworthy players for the session: Sonny Rollins (tenor sax), "Charlie Chan" (tenor sax), Walter Bishop (piano), Percy Heath (bass), and Philly Joe Jones (drums). Charlie Parker assumed the name "Charlie Chan" for this date, as he was under exclusive contract with Mercury. New to Miles' lineup was Philly Joe Jones, a drummer who would later characterize jazz drumming in the late '50s playing with Miles. The recording date was filled with difficulties and only yielded three songs: "The Serpent's Tooth" (with two takes), "'Round Midnight," and "Compulsion." Since there was not enough material to fill an LP, the songs would wait to be released with material from a recording session over three years later.

THE SERPENT'S TOOTH

From the recording *Collector's Items* (Miles Davis)

By Miles Davis

THE SERPENT'S TOOTH

KEY: B♭
FORM: AABA

B♭maj7	Bdim7	Cm7	C#dim7	Dm7	D+7	E♭m(maj7)	A♭7
I	VI7	II	VII7	III	III7	II	V / ♭VII7
	G Mix♭2(♭6)		A Mix♭2(♭6)		D Mix♭2(♭6)	D♭ Major	

B♭maj7	E7	E♭maj7	A♭7	Dm7	G7	Cm7	F7
I	♭II7	I	IV7	III	VI7	II	V
	E Mix#4		A♭ Mix#4				

B♭maj7	Bdim7	Gm7	C#dim7	Dm7	D+7	Em(maj7)	A♭7
I	VI7	II	VII7	III	III7	II	V / ♭VII7
	G Mix♭2(♭6)		A Mix♭2(♭6)	D Mix♭2(♭6)		D♭ Major	

B♭maj7	E7	E♭maj7	A♭7	B♭maj7
I	♭II7	I	IV7 / ♭VII7	I
	E Mix#4		A♭ Mix#4	

B♭7		E♭maj7	
I7		IV	
B♭ Mix			

C7		F7	
II7		V	
C Mix			

B♭maj7	Bdim7	Cm7	C#dim7	Dm7	D+7	E♭m(maj7)	A♭7
I	VI7	II	VII7	III	III7	II	V / ♭VII7
	G Mix♭2(♭6)		A Mix♭2(♭6)		D Mix♭2(♭6)	D♭ Major	

B♭maj7	E7	E♭maj7	A♭7	B♭maj7
I	♭II7	I	IV7 / ♭VII7	I
	E Mix#4		A♭ Mix#4	

Example 67: A section of "The Serpent's Tooth."

In bars 1 through 3, Miles creates an ascending chromatic line through the chords (B♭ → B → C → C♯ → D). As you can see on the analysis sheet, the two diminished chords function as secondary dominants (see page 19 for explanation). Miles makes good use of minor third substitution to get in and out of the unresolved modulation in bar 4 and the modulation in bars 5 and 6.

The V chord of the main key is F7. The minor third substitutions for F7 are A♭7, B7, and D7. In bar 3, the D7 holds out on the chromatic line that was created, ending in bar 4 on the E♭ root of E♭m7. The D7 also is the minor third substitute for A♭7, the V chord of the modulation to D♭ Major in bar 4. The A♭7 in bar 4 then splits in function as the V chord of D♭ Major and the ♭VII7 (minor third substitute for F7) in the main key of B♭ Major. This connects the A♭7 to the B♭maj7 in bar 5 as a ♭VII7 → I. In bar 6, the A♭7 ends the modulation to E♭ Major, returning to the main key in bar 7. The A♭7 has an identity in B♭ Major through minor 3rd substitution as the ♭VII7 (A♭7), ♭II7 (B7), III7 (D7), and V (F7). As Miles approached the modulation to D♭ Major in bar 4, the D7 (III7 of B♭ Major) had a minor third relationship to A♭7 (the V chord of the modulation). Then A♭7 (IV7 in the modulation to E♭ Major) had a minor third relationship to the Dm7 in bar 7, acting like a D7 → Dm7 or III7 → III.

Miles uses melodic patterns to outline the chord changes in bars 1 through 3. Each melodic pattern arpeggiates the triad of each chord played underneath. In bars 5 and 6, Miles uses an ascending chromatic line (F → F♯ → G) over a chord progression that has a descending chromatic line in it (F → E → E♭). The melody resolves to F in the first ending, acting as a chord tone for three of the four chords played underneath (3rd of Dm7, 7th of G7, root of F7). For the second ending, Miles resolves the A section to the I chord of B♭ Major, and creates a rising melody that accents the upbeats to prepare for the B section. The second ending is also used in A3 in preparation for the solos.

Example 68: B section of "The Serpent's Tooth."

Miles uses the B section as a solo section, as many of the bebop songs had (Miles used this for half of the B section in "Dig" as well). The chords are more sparse in the B section, opening room for the solo. Miles again uses secondary dominants as he had in the A section, this time creating a I7 → IV in bars 17 through 20 and a II7 → V in bars 21 through 24.

Miles' album Blue Haze *is the combination of a studio date in May of 1953 and another in March of 1954. It yielded two of Miles' best known songs: "Tune Up" and "Four." Both dates show Miles' gravitation toward the hard bop style that would characterize jazz in the mid to late '50s. Hard bop shifted the virtuosic style of bebop to more lyrical and melodic playing. The music was hardswinging and the technical flights more muscular to contrast the melodic statements in the solos. Initially, the hard bop players used the theoretical tools of bebop in their solos. But, eventually hard bop would embrace the swing-era style, bebop, and go beyond to add new elements to the jazz solo that weren't present before. With Miles melodically exploiting the color of notes over chords, and the emergence of John Coltrane's emphasis on scale substitution, the attributes of the hard bop style became clearer.*

TUNE UP

From the recordings *Blue Haze* (Miles Davis), *Cookin'* (Miles Davis)

By Miles Davis

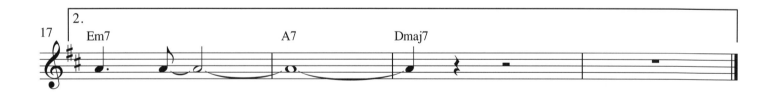

Copyright © 1963 Prestige Music
Copyright Renewed
International Copyright Secured All Rights Reserved

TUNE UP

KEY: D Major
FORM: 16 Bars

Em7	A7	Dmaj7	
II	V	I	

Dm7	G7	Cmaj7	
II	V	I	
C Major			

Cm7	F7	B♭maj7	Gm7
II	V	I	VI
B♭ Major			

1.
Em7	F7	B♭maj7	A7
II	V	I	V
	B♭ Major		

2.
Em7	A7	Dmaj7	
II	V	I	

"Tune Up" is comprised of four sections of four bars, much like an AABA which is made up of four sections of eight bars each. Each section, omitting the first ending, is essentially a II → V → I progression in its respective key. As is typical with a first ending, the chords provide a turnback to the beginning of the song, using at some point the active II and V chords. Miles adds an unexpected modulation back to B♭ Major in bars 14 and 15. The roots of the chords create a chromatic rise and fall from E to F and B♭ down to A.

Example 69: First ending of "Tune Up."

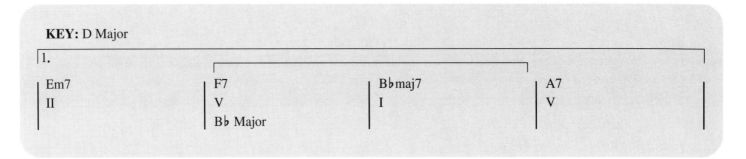

This ending was probably some of the inspiration for John Coltrane's extensive use of chord substitutions. Coltrane reworked the chords of "Tune Up" for his song "Countdown."

Example 70: Bars 1 through 4 of "Countdown."

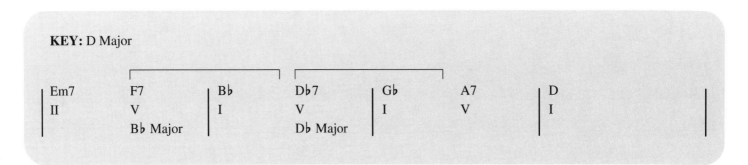

The two modulations in "Tune Up" (bars 5 through 8 to C Major and bars 9 through 12 to B♭ Major) are entered through a tonic interchange: Dmaj7 becomes Dm7 and Cmaj7 becomes Cm7.

The melody for "Tune Up" shows the move away from using chord tones in the melody on the chord changes. This was a significant shift in the hard bop period away from the trademarks of bebop. Also, notice the longer durations in the melody. The rhythms look more like those in a show tune than a bebop song.

Example 71: Bars 1 through 8 of "Tune Up."

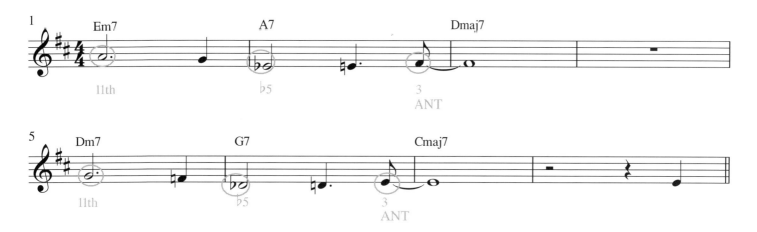

The melody begins on the 11th (A) of Em7 and moves down to the the 3rd (G). Bar 2 begins on the ♭5 (E♭) of A7 and chromatically moves to the 5th (E) and then to the anticipated (ANT) third (F♯) of Dmaj7. Bars 5 through 8 modulate to C Major and the melody in bars 1 through 4 is simply transposed to C Major. The E note on beat 4 of bar 8 allows for the melody to chromatically move into the next modulation to B♭ Major (E to E♭).

Example 72: Bars 9 through 12 of "Tune Up."

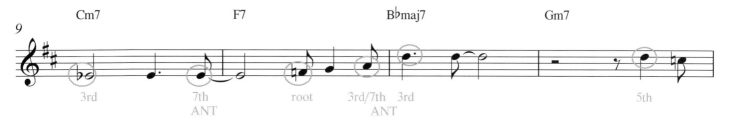

In contrast to the first motif, bars 9 through 12 create more consonance by accenting chord tones, especially the 3rd (E♭) of Cm7 and the 3rd (D) of B♭maj7.

Example 73: First and second endings of "Tune Up."

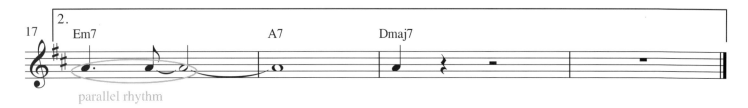

While the chords in the first ending modulate to B♭ Major for 2 bars, the melody accentuates D Major with a resolution to the 5th (A). Even the melody in bar 14, which uses the 3rd (A) and 5th (C) of F7, implies the resolution to the V chord (A7) of D Major, functioning as the root and ♯9 of A7. This is reinforced by the accented A note in bars 13 and 15, and Miles' use of C and B♭ in bar 16 (the ♯9 and ♭9 of A7).

The second ending resolves the melody to the 5th (A) of D Major, using a parallel rhythm from the first ending.

PART II | THE COMPOSITIONS

"FOUR"

"Four," like "Tune Up," is a 16-bar song with two endings. There are two main melodic motifs, one in bars 1 through 8 and the second in bars 9 through 16.

Example 74: Bars 1 through 8 of "Four."

The first motif is largely based on the repetitive three-note riff from bar 1. Bar 2 begins using the same rhythm as bar 1, descending to the D note instead of ascending in the first riff. Then, the main riff is restated using a D♭ note to anticipate the E♭m7 chord (D♭ is the 7th of E♭m7). Bars 5 through 7 shift the melody of bars 1 through 3 up a fourth. This time the melody ends on the anticipated 7th (G♭) of A♭m7. The melody in bar 8 prepares for the next motif using a chromatic passing tone (A) to connect the A♭ to a B♭.

Miles establishes two modulations in these first 8 bars. In the first modulation to D♭ Major, Miles uses a tonic interchange to enter the modulation (E♭maj7 becomes E♭m7). The V chord (A♭7) of the modulation is the partial diatonic IV7 chord of E♭ Major and allows Miles to re-enter the main key in bar 5. The three-note riff in bar 1 outlines the E♭maj7 chord using its 5th and 7th chord tones (B♭ and D). When the melody shifts in bar 5, it seems to again outline the E♭maj7 chord using its root and 3rd (E♭ and G). However, Miles uses the active II chord (Fm7) under the melody, giving an added momentum to the song.

85

FOUR

From the recordings *Blue Haze* (Miles Davis), *Workin'* (Miles Davis),
The Complete Concert 1964 (My Funny Valentine + Four & More) (Miles Davis)

By Miles Davis

Copyright © 1963 Prestige Music
Copyright Renewed
International Copyright Secured All Rights Reserved

FOUR

KEY: E♭ Major
FORM: 16 Bars

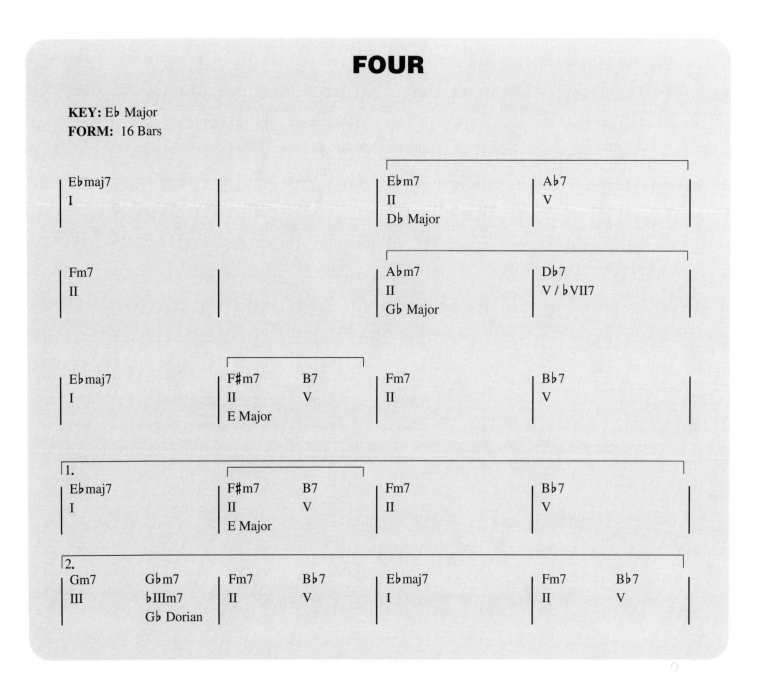

The modulation in bar 7 is entered with an A♭m7 chord. There are two ways to look at the use of the modulation:

1. The A♭m7 is a minor 3rd away from Fm7 and, in effect, acts as a minor 3rd substitution. Then the V chord (D♭7) splits its function, becoming the ♭VII7 (or minor 3rd substitute for the V chord) in the main key, resolving to the I chord in bar 9.

2. This is a more exaggerated way of viewing the modulation, but will help you understand chord relationships and connection. Let's assume for a moment that bars 5 through 8 were a II → V progression in the main key of E♭ Major.

Example 75:

Fm7		B♭7	
II		V	

Using minor 3rd substitution, the V chord (B♭7) can be substituted with a D♭7 chord.

Example 76:

Fm7		D♭7	
II		♭VII7	

Using direct substitution, any active chord can be substituted for another active chord. Treating D♭7 as a V chord (in G♭ Major), it can be substituted with the II chord (A♭m7), which brings us to the progression Miles used in "Four."

Example 77:

Fm7		A♭m7	D♭7
II		II	V
		G♭ Major	

Example 78: Bars 9 through 16 of "Four."

The chords and melody in bars 9 through 12 are basically repeated in bars 13 through 16, with a minor change in the melody. The chord progression is a II → V → (I) in the main key (E♭ Major). Miles adds a chromatic modulation in bar 14 to E Major, chromatically lifting the key from E♭ to E♮ and back down to E♭. The melody in bar 9 outlines the E♭maj7 chord it is played over, using chord tones (root, 3rd, and 5th). The B♮ on the upbeat of 4 chromatically moves up from B♭, anticipating the chromatic modulation to E Major. As was stated earlier, an active chord can substitute for another active chord. So it is common in a II → V progression for a soloist to play only over the II chord or only over the V chord. In bar 10, Miles stresses a D♯ and (as this melody repeated in bar 13) a B♮. These are the chord tone 3rd and root of B7, so Miles is emphasizing the V chord over the II chord. Bar 11 emphasizes the chord tones of Fm7 (C and A♭) and anticipates the B7 chord with its 13th (G). This is Miles' first use of an upper partial on a chord change in "Four" (unlike "Tune Up", which readily used upper partials and alterations in the melody). The rhythm at the end of bar 12 mirrors the riff used in bar 1. In bars 13 through 16, Miles uses the motif of bars 9 through 12, accentuating the B♮ in bar 14, and using an E♮ to chromatically push down to the D♯.

Example 79: Second ending of "Four."

Miles reworked the chords of the first ending to create a new progression in the second ending. The G♭m7 is the direct passive substitute for the Emaj7 in the first ending (III for I). The G♭m7 is enharmonically F♯m7. Miles again uses the II and V chords of E♭ Major (Fm7 → B♭7) and ends the song on the I chord (E♭maj7). The result of this progression is a chromatic line between the first three chords (G → G♭ → F), and yet he maintains some of the identity of the first ending's progression.

The melody of the second ending begins on a B♭ note much as the first ending had. This time, though, Miles creates an ascending line within the melody to give way to the end of the song and the beginning of the solo. The melody uses chord tones to outline each chord it is played over, with the exception of the G♭m7. If you remember in the first ending, Miles used B♮, E♮ and D♯ in the melody to accentuate the B7, not the F♯m7. In the second ending, Miles uses C♭, F♭, and E♭ over the G♭m7. This is enharmonically the B♮, E♮, and D♯ of the first ending, so Miles is essentially still responding to the B7 chord.

In December of 1954, Miles entered the studio with Milt Jackson (vibes), Thelonius Monk (piano), Pearcy Heath (bass), and Kenny Clarke (drums). The result was an exceptional session, with the standout playing that Miles was slowly becoming known for. His one original for the date was "Swing Spring." Both "Swing Spring" and "Solar," from an earlier date, were recorded and left behind by Miles. Despite that, the songs remained popular due to other players renditions of the songs.

PART II | THE COMPOSITIONS

"SWING SPRING"

"Swing Spring" is an AABA form with basically one theme.

Example 80: A section of "Swing Spring."

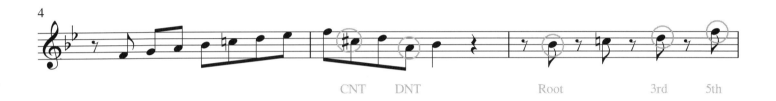

Although there is one chord for the A section, it is listed repeatedly according to where it is actually played on the recording. The theme for "Swing Spring" is stated in bars 1 and 2. This is a bebop line that begins on the 5th (F) of the I chord (B♭maj) and ascends the B♭ Major scale an octave to F. Bar 2 arpeggiates the B♭ triad and adds a neighbor tone, which moves into each chord tone. The C♯ note moves by one half step into the D (the 3rd of B♭maj), making the C♯ a chromatic neighbor tone (CNT), because C♯ is chromatic to the key of B♭ Major. Similarly, the A note moves by one half step into B♭ (the root of B♭maj). This time the A note is diatonic to B♭ Major, making it a diatonic neighbor tone (DNT). Miles shortens the theme in bar 4, and lengthens it in bar 8, using the E♮ as a chromatic neighbor tone to move by one half step to the F note (the 5th of B♭maj). Bar 5 adds some rhythmic flare to the original theme. The scale run in bars 1 and 2 is reduced to include mostly chord tones (B♭, D, and F), and every upbeat in the bar is accented.

SWING SPRING

From the recording *Miles Davis and the Modern Jazz Giants* (Miles Davis)

By Miles Davis

SWING SPRING

KEY: B♭ Major
Form: AABA

B♭/F		B♭/F	
I		I	

B♭/F		B♭/F	
I		I	

B♭/F		B♭/F	
I		I	

B♭/F		B♭/F	
I		I	

B♭m7	A7	A♭m7	G7
II	♭II7	II	♭II7
A♭ Major	A Mix♯4	G♭ Major	G Mix♯4

Gm7	G♭7	Fm7	F7
II	♭II7	II	V
F Major	G♭ Mix♯4	E♭ Major	

B♭/F		B♭/F	
I		I	

B♭/F		B♭/F	
I		I	

Example 81: Section B of "Swing Spring."

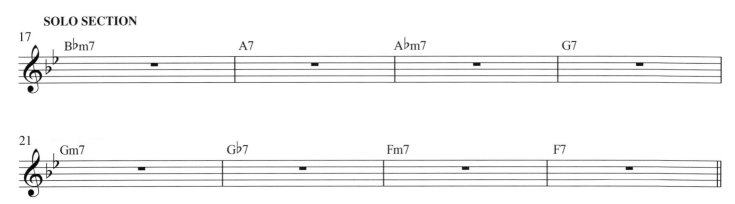

Miles again uses the B section as a solo section instead of using a written melody. For the chord progression, he sets up four chromatic modulations which create a chromatic line through the B section [B♭ → A → A♭ → G → (G) → G♭ → F → (F)]. The first three modulations are all II → ♭II7 progressions in their respective keys (the ♭II7 acting as the tritone substitute for the V chord). Miles enters and exits each modulation with the use of an interchange. Bars 17 and 18 are in A♭ Major, and the II → ♭II7 progression expects a resolution to the tonic chord, A♭maj7. Instead, Miles uses A♭m7 as the tonic interchange for A♭maj7, setting up the next modulation to G♭ Major. The modulation to G♭ major similarly ends on the ♭II7 chord (G7). This time Miles uses Gm7 as an interchange for G7 to begin the modulation to F Major. The Fm7 in bar 23 acts as the interchange for Fmaj7, which would have resolved the previous modulation to F Major. Then, the F7 in bar 24 acts as the interchange for Fm7, bringing the song back to the main key of B♭ Major.

By 1955, Miles had recorded many albums for Prestige. The results of the sessions seemed to widely vary from incredible performances to dispassionate song renditions. Critical acclaim seemed to elude Miles, and the listening public was still waiting to be overwhelmed. All of this would seemingly change overnight for Miles. In July of 1955, he appeared at the first annual Newport Jazz Festival. His solo performance on "Round Midnight," played with Thelonius Monk, astounded the fans and critics. The talk and exposure that would ensue from this performance would label this as Miles' "comeback," and send his career down a path of greater opportunity and stardom.

By fall of 1955, Miles had completed a few more recording dates, but he was still trying to establish a working band. Miles put together a quintet to satisfy some club dates, and as it turned out he found a group of players that could achieve the sound he was looking for. The quintet included John Coltrane (tenor sax), Red Garland (piano), Paul Chambers (bass), and Philly Joe Jones (drums). Each of these players would come to epitomize the style and sound of their instruments and set the standard of excellence by which all others would be measured.

The new quintet immediately caught the attention of fans and critics. Columbia Records approached Miles with a very lucrative contract that would allow the quintet the money and exposure they deserved. The only obstacle was the contract with Prestige that Miles was already obligated to fulfill. Miles immediately began recording to fulfill the Prestige contract, and privately recorded the material that would end up on his first

Columbia LP, *Round About Midnight*. *The Prestige contract stipulated that Miles deliver a certain amount of material, at which time the contract would end. In two long sessions (May 11, 1956 and October 26, 1956) Miles recorded enough material with the quintet to end the Prestige contract. These studio sessions ran much like a club date, with the band playing one song after another and usually the first take was the only take. The combined result of these sessions yielded four exceptional LPs for Prestige: Workin', Steamin', Relaxin', and Cookin'.*

BLUES BY FIVE

From the recording *Cookin'* (Miles Davis)

By Red Garland

Copyright © 1965 Prestige Music
Copyright Renewed
International Copyright Secured   All Rights Reserved

BLUES BY FIVE

KEY: B♭ Major
FORM: Blues

B♭7			
I			
B♭ Mix			

E♭7		B♭7	
I		I	
E♭ Mix		B♭ Mix	

F7		B♭ G7♭9	Cm7 F7♭9
V		I VI7	II V
		B♭ Mix G Mix♭2(♭6)	

Example 82: "Blues by Five."

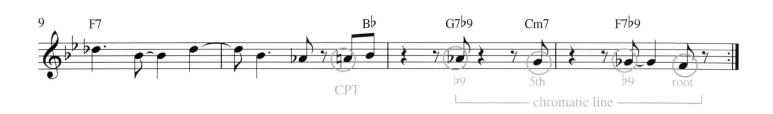

"Blues by Five" is a basic blues (see page 37) with a turnback in bars 11 and 12 (I → VI7 → II → V). For the melody, Miles works almost exclusively with the blues scale. The blues scale is developed from a minor chord using the root, third, fourth, fifth, and seventh. The B♭ Blues scale is based on B♭m7: B♭ (root), D♭ (3rd), E♭ (4th), F (5th), and A♭ (7th). A blues scale can also be played over a 7th chord (B♭7) because the minor 3rd (D♭) acts as the ♯9 (C♯), while the other four notes maintain a diatonic function: B♭ (root), E♭ (4th), F (5th), and A♭ (7th). In bar 1 of "Blues by Five," Miles establishes the main motif using the B♭ Blues scale. The melody moves from F (5th) to A♭ (7th) to B♭ (root) and back to F (5th). In bar 5, the melody is transposed to fit over the E♭7 chord, and in doing so uses the E♭ Blues scale. In bars 9 and 10, Miles continues using the B♭ Blues scale over the V chord (F7): D♭ (3rd/♯9) → B♭ (root) → D♭ (3rd/♯9) → B♭ (root) → A♭ (7th). A chromatic passing tone (CPT), the A♮ note, connects A♭ to B♭ ending the main theme on the root of the I chord (B♭7). In the turnback, Miles creates a chromatic line using chord tones and alterations from the chords played underneath.

1957 saw the first of several collaborations between Miles and Gil Evans. Gil Evans had been an important influence on the nonet recording for Birth of the Cool, *and contributed some arrangements to the* Round About Midnight *LP. Now, Gil Evans would provide arrangements for a nineteen-piece orchestra where Miles would be the featured soloist. Many jazz players had recorded songs or standards with an orchestra before* Charlie Parker with Strings, *for example, and this was by no means a new vehicle for a jazz soloist. The orchestral arrangements for these types of albums typically would mimic the piano accompaniment in a small group, for the soloist to play over. Gil Evans, however, delivered arrangements that were in many ways the song itself. His unique approach to chord voicings and instrument arrangements set a new standard of excellence for jazz orchestral albums. These magnificent arrangements were in no way intended for the aggressive and complicated playing of most jazz players, though. Miles ability to play within the arrangements and not over them, was a talent that was always unmistakably his. By now, Miles' solo style embodied space, sensitivity, and unique note choice. All of these elements combined with Evans' arrangements to create masterpieces. Their orchestral collaborations continued through 1962, recording four albums that have become some of Miles' best-known work:* Miles Ahead *(1957),* Porgy and Bess *(1958),* Sketches of Spain *(1959), and* Quiet Nights *(1962).*

"MILES AHEAD"

"Miles Ahead" is somewhat reminiscent of the cool jazz Miles and Gil Evans created seven years earlier. The song is taken at a slow tempo, and the repetitive use of quarter-note triplets keeps the rhythm sounding laid back while establishing a rhythmic motif.

MILES AHEAD

KEY: C Major

	G7 V	Cmaj7 I		

| Dm7
II | Em7
III | Dm7
II | Gm7
II
F Major | |

| | Fmaj7
I | | Bb7
IV7
Bb Mix#4 | |

| E7
V
A HM | Am7   Am7/G
I
A NM | F#m7b5   F7
II   bII7
E HM   F Mix#4 | Em7b5
II
D HM | |

| A7
V | Dm7
I
D NM | | Cmaj7
I | |

| Dm7
II | Em7
III | Dm7
II | Gm7
II
F Major | |

| Fmaj7
I | | Bm7b5
II
A HM | E7
V | |

| Em7b5
II
D HM | | A7
V | Dm7
I
D HM | |

Example 83: Bars 1 through 8 of "Miles Ahead."

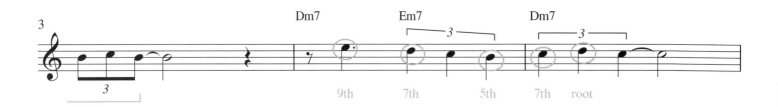

In bars 1 through 6, Miles establishes the main theme, which is repeated in bars 17 through 22. The entire melody makes strong use of chord tones and the ninths of the chords played underneath. In bar 6, Miles establishes a modulation to the key of the IV chord (F Major). He enters the key of F Major using the II chord (Gm7). The Gm7 has a strong connection to Dm7, but not through the relationship of either keys C Major or F Major. If the Dm7 is heard as the I chord in D Minor, then the Gm7 would act as the IV chord. Certainly the Gm7 played over 3 bars adds to the ambiguity of the new key, until it resolves to Fmaj7 (the I chord of the new modulation) in bar 9.

Example 84: Bars 9 through 16 of "Miles Ahead."

The melody for this part of the song makes even more use of upper partials and adds some alterations, most notably the #11. While the melody does not use repetitive structures, the sustained rhythms reinforce the mood and laid-back feel of the entire melody. In bar 11, Mile ends the modulation to F Major with a B♭7 chord, the IV7 chord. Making the IV chord a IV7 (a device often used by earlier writers like George Gershwin and Duke Ellington) is a common application of the blues. The B♭7 also sets up the next modulation to A Minor. The chords move from B♭7 to E7, which is the tritone substitute for B♭7, and the E7 becomes the V chord in A Minor.

Example 85: Chord analysis of bars 12 through 29 of "Miles Ahead."

KEY: C Major

E7	Am7 Am7/G	F#m7b5 F7	Em7b5
V	I	II bII7	II
	(IV in E Minor)	(tritone substitute)	(interchange for Em7)

A7	Dm7		Cmaj7
V	I		I
	(II chord in C Major)		

Dm7 Em7	Dm7	Gm7	
II III	II	II	
	(VI chord in F Major)		

Fmaj7	Bm7b5	E7	
I	II	V	
(VI chord in A Minor)			

Em7b5	A7	Dm7	
II	V	I	
(interchange for E7)			

Example 85 expands on the original analysis sheet and shows the way each modulation is entered and exited. Miles' use of modulation and chord connection is more extensive than the previous song reviewed. There is a certain amount of subtlety involved in the chord progression of "Miles Ahead," where the keys smoothly flow in and out of each other due to their chord relationships. This is also partially due to Gil Evans' beautiful arrangement of the song, which aids in the flow of the chords.

Example 86: Bars 25 through 29 of "Miles Ahead."

This is the final excerpt of "Miles Ahead," which completes the main melodic theme. The song continues with new chord progressions and allows for improvisation from Miles. As with the previous measure of "Miles Ahead," Miles uses upper partials and alterations on the chord changes, adding more color to the overall song. As you look at the entire excerpt on page 98, notice how the melody stays in the main key of C Major throughout. If this song were written in the style of a show tune, you could see how the melody indicates chords in C Major or the relative minor (A Minor). The brilliance of "Miles Ahead" lies in Miles' ability to use so many modulations under a C Major melody. The careful use of the melody notes as chord tones, upper partials, and alterations over a well-connected chord progression gives "Miles Ahead" the feeling of movement and color without being forced.

In 1958, Miles added the talent of Julian "Cannonball" Adderly to his group. Adderly had been a music teacher in Florida, and he spent his summers breaking into the New York jazz scene. Already known in jazz circles, Adderly had made recordings as a leader before becoming a member of Miles' band (one which included a date with Miles' Somethin' Else). *His unique voice on the alto saxophone and predilection for the blues complimented and contrasted the styles of Miles and John Coltrane. The new Miles Davis sextet recorded another landmark album in April of 1958:* Milestones.

MILES

From the recording *Milestones* (Miles Davis)

By Miles Davis

MILES

KEY: G Dorian
FORM: AABA

| Gm7 | Am7 | B♭maj7 | Am7 | Gm7 | Am7 | B♭maj7 | Am7 |
| I | II | III | II | I | II | III | II |

| Gm7 | Am7 | B♭maj7 | Gm7 | Am7 | | | |
| I | II | III | I | II | | | |

| Gm7 | Am7 | B♭maj7 | Am7 | Gm7 | Am7 | B♭maj7 | Am7 |
| I | II | III | II | I | II | III | II |

| Gm7 | Am7 | B♭maj7 | Gm7 | Am7 | | | |
| I | II | III | I | II | | | |

Am7	16
I	
A Dorian	

| Gm7 | Am7 | B♭maj7 | Am7 | Gm7 | Am7 | B♭maj7 | Am7 |
| I | II | III | II | II | III | II | |

| Gm7 | Am7 | B♭maj7 | Gm7 | Am7 | | | |
| I | II | III | I | I | | | |

THE MUSIC OF MILES DAVIS

"Miles" – more commonly known as "Milestones" – is Miles' first song entirely written using modes. The piece marked his gravitation not only toward modality, but his preference for fewer chords in a song. Unlike John Coltrane who was experimenting with the effect of different scales over chords and chord substitution in his solos, Miles would exploit the use of one or two notes over a chord to express color and tension. The use of fewer chords naturally played into Miles' unique solo style.

Example 87: A section of "Miles."

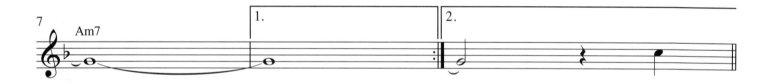

Section A is in G Dorian, and uses one motif. The I, II, and III chords in G Dorian are used to follow the theme, with each melody note acting as the chord tone 7th of each chord.

Example 88: B Section, bars 17 through 24 of "Miles."

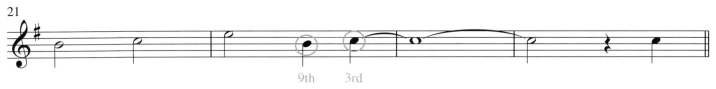

The B section modulates to A Dorian. This section theme is basically a variation on the melody of the A section. Miles opens up the B section melody using half notes and ends the chord movement created in the A section by using a bass pedal. The B section (at 16 bars) is double the length of the A section. The first 8 bars of the B section are repeated exactly in the second 8 bars.

Following the recording of Milestones, *Red Garland and Philly Joe Jones were replaced by Bill Evans and Jimmy Cobb. Bill Evans, much like Adderly, was becoming known as a leader, recording in a trio format under his own name. Bill Evan's distinctive piano style, and influences that ranged from classical composers to jazz players like Bud Powell, had a profound effect on Miles and his band. Evans', like Miles, had a great feel for space and sensitivity in his playing, and had a remarkable way of voicing and using voice-leading chords. His stay with Miles as a working band member lasted only eight months, but he did return to record the album* Kind of Blue.

During Evan's stay with Miles, he played on Julian Adderly's album Portrait of Cannonball. *One of the songs recorded for the date was Miles' song "Nardis." "Nardis" was never recorded by Miles himself, but went on to become a favorite of Bill Evans. Evans recorded the song many times with his trios, and the transformation of the song over the years from the Adderly album is quite impressive.*

NARDIS

From the recordings *Portrait of Cannonball* (Cannonball Adderly),
You're Gonna Hear from Me (Bill Evans), *Bill Evans at the Montreux Jazz Festival* (Bill Evans), *Turn out the Stars* (Bill Evans),
The Secret Sessions (Bill Evans)

By Miles Davis

Copyright © 1959 Jazz Horn Music
Copyright Renewed
All Rights Administered by Sony/ATV Music Publishing, 8 Music Square West, Nashville, TN 37203
International Copyright Secured   All Rights Reserved

NARDIS

KEY: E minor
FORM: AABA

Em7	Fmaj7 Ebmaj7	Bm7	Cmaj7
I	bIImaj7 Imaj7	V	VI
E NM	F Lydian E Major	E HM	E NM

Am7	Fmaj7	Emaj7	Em7
IV	bIImaj7	Imaj7	I
	F Lydian	E Major	E NM

Em7	Fmaj7 Emaj7	B7	Cmaj7
I	bIImaj7 Imaj7	V	VI
E NM	F Lydian E Major	E HM	E NM

Am7	Fmaj7	Emaj7	Em7
IV	bIImaj7	Imaj7	I
	F Lydian	E Major	E NM

Am7	Fmaj7	Am7	Fmaj7
IV	bIImaj7	IV	
E NM	F Lydian	E NM	

Dm7	G7	Cmaj7	Fmaj7
II	V	I	IV/bIImaj7
C Major			F Lydian

Em7	Fmaj7 Emaj7	B7	Cmaj7
I	bIImaj7 Imaj7	V	VI
E NM	F Lydian E Major	E HM	E NM

Am7	Fmaj7	Emaj7	Em7
IV	bIImaj7	Imaj7	I
	F Lydian	E Major	E NM

Example 89: A section of "Nardis."

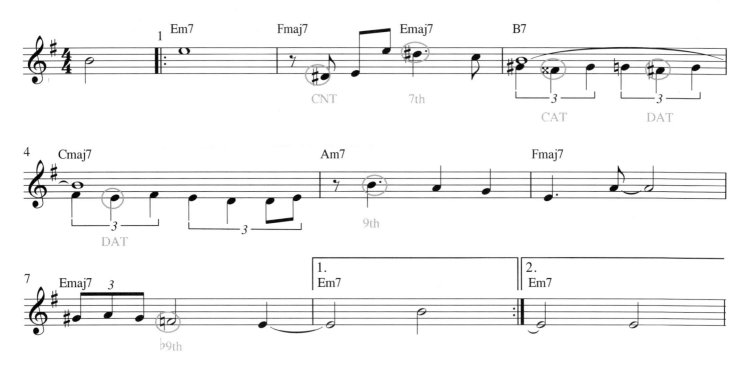

This version of "Nardis" includes Bill Evans' counter line in bars 3 and 4, against the original sustained B note. The entire A section is in E Minor, and makes strong use of a tonic interchange (Emaj7 for Em7). Miles also uses Fmaj7 as a minor 3rd substitute for the V chord (B7). This was becoming more popular in jazz, replacing the bII7 chord with a bIImaj7 for a more colorful effect. The resolution to the major I chord is then entirely chromatic, which supports Miles' use of the tonic interchange.

Example 90:

Fmaj7 (bIImaj7)	resolves to	Emaj7 (Imaj7)
F	one half step down	E
A	one half step down	G#
C	one half step down	B
E	one half step down	D#

In bar 2, Miles melodically uses a D# note as a chromatic neighbor tone to E♮, which is at once the 7th of Fmaj7 and the root of Emaj7. The D# on beat 3 then becomes the chord-tone 7th of Emaj7. The B♮ in bars 3 and 4 connect the B7 and Cmaj7, acting as the root of B7 and the 7th of Cmaj7. Bill Evans added a counter line in bars 3 and 4 to give some melodic movement. Each quarter-note triplet uses an auxilary tone. An auxilary tone connects a note back to itself by use of a note that is either diatonic (DAT) or chromatic (CAT) to the key. In the first quarter-note triplet the F## is chromatic to E Minor (and E Major), making this a chromatic auxilary tone. Bill Evans adds a nice twist to the melody, treating the first quarter-note triplet as part of E Major and the second as part of E Minor (due to the use of G# and G♮ in the melody). This works well because B7 is the V chord in both E Minor and E Major. Since Miles used a tonic interchange in bar 2 (Emaj7), Evans begins the melody as if B7 were in E Major. Then he drifts back to E Minor (using a G♮) to anticipate the Cmaj7 in bar 4, which is clearly the VI chord in E Minor. In bar 5, Miles uses the 9th (B) of Am7 to begin the melody. As is readily apparent in Miles' earlier songs, the hard bop period made use of upper partials and alterations on the chord changes, whereas this was more of an exception in bebop. In bar 7, the F♮ gives the melody a harmonic minor flavor with the minor 3rd interval between G♯ and F♮. The F♮ functions as the ♭9 over Emaj7 and adds some tension to the melody, which is waiting to resolve to E♮ (the root of E Minor).

Example 91: B section of "Nardis."

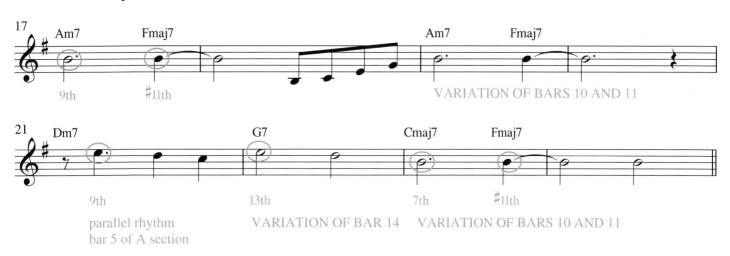

Unlike the A section which uses all 8 bars to establish the theme, the B section stresses only one motif. This motif is established in bars 1 and 2, and again makes use of upper partials and alterations. Bars 5 and 6 connect the B theme to the A theme with melodic and rhythmic references. Bars 5 through 8 provide the only modulation of the song to C Major. Miles shows some of his ingenuity from "Miles Ahead" in this modulation. The progression from Am7 to Dm7 has two relationships. First, an Am7 can be a I chord in A Minor progressing to the IV chord (Dm7). Second, the Am7 can be the VI chord in C Major progressing to the II chord (Dm7). By the time the G7 is played, it is clear the modulation has entered C Major. The final chord of the modulation (Fmaj7) splits its function as the IV chord in C Major and as the previously established function of a ♭IImaj7 in E Minor, which brings the B section back to the A section.

Kind of Blue is perhaps Miles' best-known album and stands out as one of the defining moments in jazz. At the time it was recorded, Coltrane, Adderly, and Evans were all becoming important band leaders under their own names. While all-star albums were commonplace in jazz, bringing together big names for a recording session, none were perhaps as dynamic as this band. Apart from having four distinctive leaders on the date (Miles, Coltrane, Adderly, and Evans), each were working members of Miles' band. The result of having so many extremely talented leaders and players that have all played together regularly is profound. Kind of Blue *yielded five songs all composed by Miles. "So What," "Freddie Freeloader," "Blue in Green," "All Blues," and "Flamenco Sketches." "Blue in Green" and "Flamenco Sketches" notably bear the mark of Bill Evans' style in the songs. Each song was either written out or presented as a loose sketch*

THE MUSIC OF MILES DAVIS

to the other players for the first time at the recording session. As was becoming common for Miles, each song was completed in one take, with the exception of "Flamenco Sketches" in two takes. The strength of the solos and interaction of the band is exceptional for only one take and epitomize Miles' gifts as a leader.

"So What" is probably the best-known modal song in jazz. While it was far from the first example of modality in jazz, "So What" seemed to spark the widespread use of modality by other players. The song is set up as an AABA form, with the B section modulating the melody and chords up a half step from D Dorian to E♭ Dorian.

Example 92: A section of "So What."

The main motif is established in the pickup bar, and variations are played in bars 2 and 4. Bar 6 adds some variety to the melody and completes the entire theme. Each time the main motif is stated, a II → I chord progression follows. Notice how each chord is voiced largely as a quartal chord (see page 17 for explanation).

112

PART II | THE COMPOSITIONS

SO WHAT

From the recording *Kind of Blue* (Miles Davis),
The Complete Concert 1964 (My Funny Valentine + Four & More) (Miles Davis)

By Miles Davis

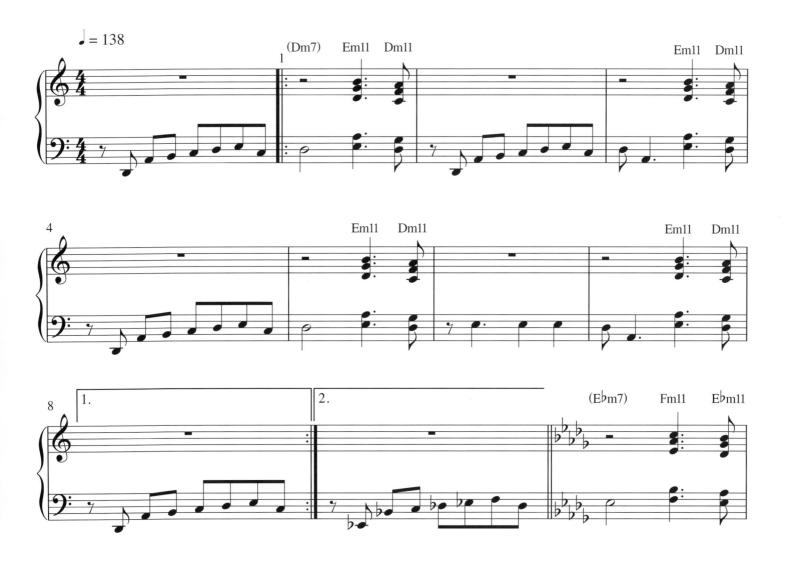

Copyrigth © 1959 Jazz Horn Music
Copyright Renewed
All Rights Administered by Sony/ATV Music Publishing, 8 Music Square West, Nashville, TN 37203
International Copyright Secured   All Rights Reserved

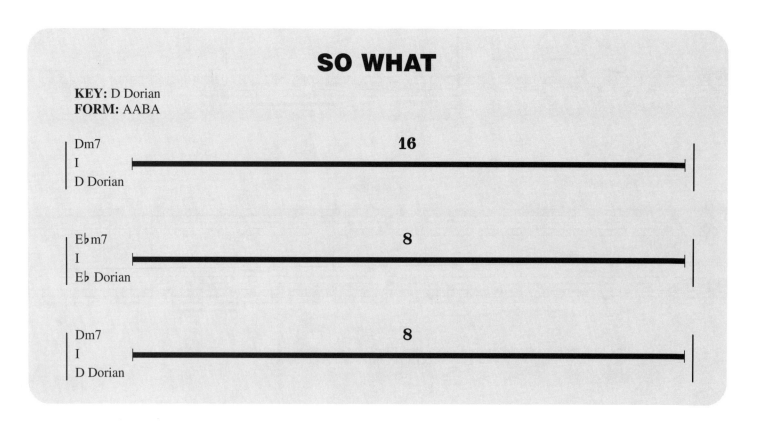

"FREDDIE FREELOADER"

"Freddie Freeloader" is the only song on *Kind of Blue* that Miles replaced Bill Evans on piano with Wynton Kelly. Bill Evans had a soft touch, and Miles used Wynton Kelly for a more aggressive approach to this blues. "Freddie Freeloader" is almost completely a basic blues. Miles added a IV7 chord in bar 10 in support of the descending melody. Also, in bars 11 and 12 of the first ending, he replaces the normal I chord with a ♭VII7 chord. The ♭VII7 is the minor 3rd substitute for the V chord (F7) and adds tension to the turnback, awaiting the I chord in bar 1.

Example 93: "Freddie Freeloader"

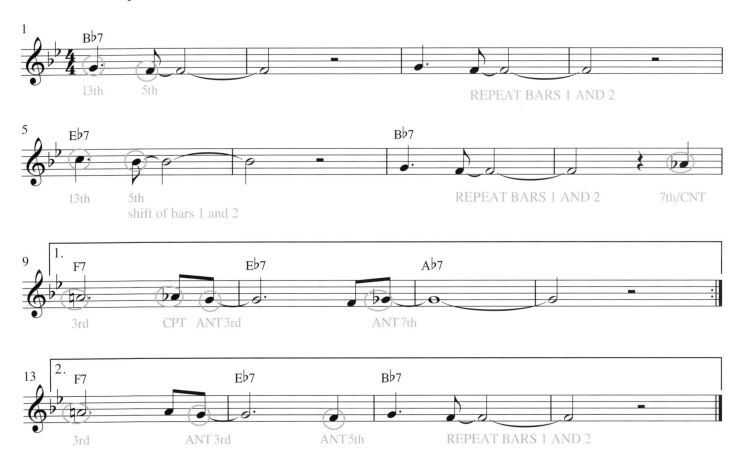

As by now was commonplace for Miles, many of the melody notes on the chord changes were upper partials. The melody for "Freddie Freeloader" is mostly comprised of the motif in bars 1 and 2. The motif begins with the color tone 13th (G) and ends with the more consonant 5th (F). In bar 8, the A♭ note acts as both the 7th of B♭7 and as a chromatic neighbor tone to the A♮ in bar 9. The A♭ is re-emphasized as a chromatic passing tone in bar 9, connecting the A♮ to the G♮. This was a very common sequence in bebop, and Miles gets a lot of color out of it in this medium-tempo blues. The chromaticism is again exaggerated in the melody as the sustained G♮ eventually moves to the G♭ in bars 11 and 12. Notice, too, how Miles uses more chord tones in the melody for the ending, to close out the theme.

FREDDIE FREELOADER
From the recording *Kind of Blue* (Miles Davis)

By Miles Davis

Copyright © 1959 Jazz Horn Music
Copyright Renewed
All Rights Administered by Sony/ATV Music Publishing, 8 Music Square West, Nashville, TN 37203
International Copyright Secured · All Rights Reserved

FREDDIE FREELOADER

KEY: B♭ Major
FORM: Blues

B♭7				
I				
B♭ Mix				

E♭7		B♭7		
IV		I		
E♭ Mix		B♭ Mix		

1.

F7	E♭7	A♭7		
V	IV	♭VII7		
	E♭ Mix	A♭ Mix♯4		

2.

F7	E♭7	B♭7		
V	IV	I		
	E♭ Mix	B♭ Mix		

FLAMENCO SKETCHES

From the recording *Kind of Blue* (Miles Davis)

By Miles Davis

Copyright © 1959 Jazz Horn Music
Copyright Renewed
All Rights Administered by Sony/ATV Music Publishing, 8 Music Square West, Nashville, TN 37203
International Copyright Secured All Rights Reserved

FLAMENCO SKETCHES

KEY: C Major
FORM: 24 Bars

Cmaj9	Dm7/G	Cmaj9	Dm7/G	Cmaj9	Dm7/G	Cmaj9	Ab/Eb
I	II	I	II	I	II	I	I
							Ab Major

Gb/Ab	Ab/Eb	Gb/Ab	Ab/Eb	Gb/Ab	Ab/Eb	Gb/Ab	F7
bVIImaj7	I	bVIImaj7	I	bVIImaj7	I	bVIImaj7	V
Gb Lydian		Gb Lydian		Gb Lydian		Gb Lydian	Bb Major

Bbmaj9	Eb/F	Bbmaj9	Eb/F	Bbmaj9	Eb/F	Bbmaj9	
I	IV	I	IV	I	IV	I	

D	Eb/D	D	Eb/D	D	Eb/D	D	Eb/D
I	bIImaj7	I	bIImaj7	I	bIImaj7	I	bIImaj7
*(D Phrygian)							

D	Eb/D	D	Eb/D	D	Eb/D	D	D7#9
I	bIImaj7	I	bIImaj7	I	bIImaj7	I	V
							G HM

Gm7				
I				
G NM				

*In this section the accompanist uses the D Phrygian Major scale for the chords, while the soloist uses the D Phrygian scale.

"Flamenco Sketches" is somewhat the outgrowth of Bill Evans' song "Peace Piece," which he recorded in December of 1958. "Peace Piece" begins exactly the same as "Flamenco Sketches," with a two-chord progression in C Major. At some point Miles and possibly Evans (as there is a great amount of controversy who actually wrote "Flamenco Sketches" and "Blue in Green") added four more modulations to the two-chord progression of "Peace Piece." The mood and feel of "Flamenco Sketches" is the same as "Peace Piece," but the added modulations give the song some added depth and color.

The chord voicings for the progressions are distinctly Evans and add a great deal to the dynamics of the song. As Evans indicated in the liner notes for Kind of Blue, *"Flamenco Sketches" is not only constructed of five distinctive keys, but five distinct scales that are used by the soloists. The goal of using only specific scales is to illicit a more melodic solo from each player, much as "So What" accomplished using only two modes. "Flamenco Sketches" has no melody, instead allowing Miles' playing at the beginning of the song to be freely improvised. With the reissue of* Kind of Blue *and the alternate take of "Flamenco Sketches," it is abundantly clear how there is no predetermined melody, with Miles playing a much different solo in the beginning of the song.*

Example 94: *Bars 1 through 4 of "Flamenco Sketches."*

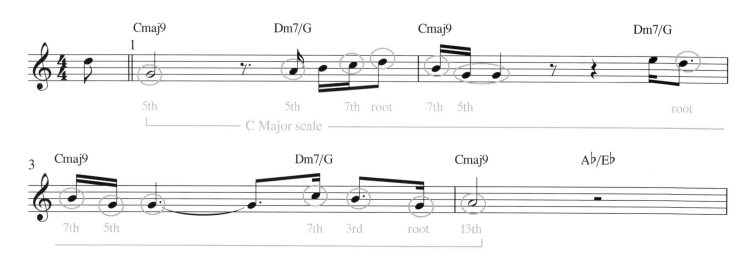

The first chord progression is in C Major and the soloist's scale choice is also C Major. Some color is added to the I chord with the addition of the ninth, a preferred choice of upper partials in Bill Evans' playing. The active II chord is always placed on beat 4 and offers a softer resolution to the I chord than the V chord, because there is no tritone in the II chord. To add some push to the progression, a G bass is added to the Dm7 (II chord), providing a V → I resolution in the bass, but a II → I resolution in the chords. Miles uses chord tones in his solo and emphasizes the G note as sort of a motif in the first 4 bars. As is true of all of "Flamenco Sketches," Miles plays only notes from the predetermined scales for the song, avoiding any chromaticism or alterations.

Example 95: Bars 5 through 8 of "Flamenco Sketches."

This progression is more ambiguous than the other four progressions. The bass maintains the 5th to root resolution/theme that was established in bars 1 through 4. The chords, however, do the opposite of the bass. When the 5th of A♭ major (E♭) is in the bass, the resolutional I chord (A♭maj) is played over the top. When the bass resolves to the root of A♭ Major (A♭), the active ♭VII chord (G♭maj) is played over the top (the ♭VII being the minor 3rd substitute for the V chord). The G♭ chord is extended to G♭maj7 on the analysis sheet because of the repetitive use of F♮ (the maj7 of G♭) in Miles' solo. The scale used for this section is a five-note scale using the notes B♭, D♭, E♭, F, and A♭. The scale fits nicely over G♭maj7 (G♭ B♭ D♭ F) and A♭maj7 (A♭ C E♭ G), avoiding the conflicting G♮ and G♭ of the two chords. This five-note scale is listed as a B♭ Blues scale in the previous example, as it is the blues scale of the II chord (B♭m7) in A♭ Major.

Example 96: Bars 9 through 12 of "Flamenco Sketches."

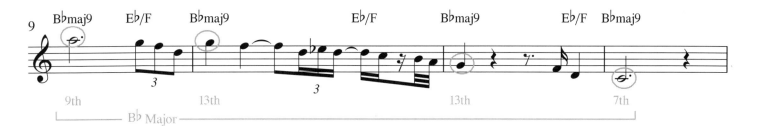

This section modulate to B♭ Major. The I chord is again extended to include the 9th (B♭maj9). The IV chord (E♭) is placed on beat 4 which resolves back to the I chord. The bass maintains the 5th to root resolution/theme. Miles uses a B♭ Major scale in his solo, emphasizing upper partials on the chord changes.

Example 97: Bars 13 through 20 of "Flamenco Sketches."

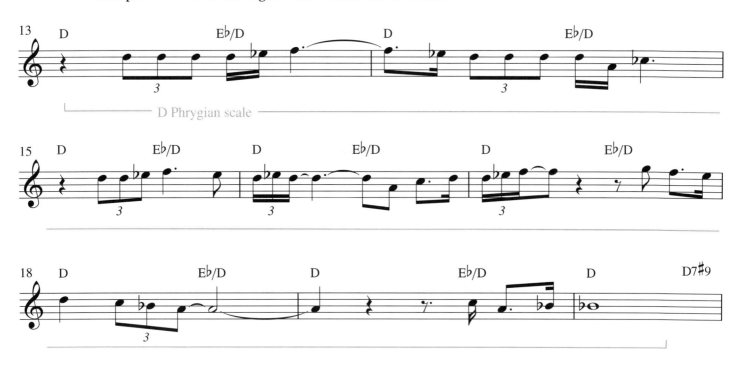

This modulation moves into D Phrygian Major (see page 29 for explanation). Bill Evans alternates between the I and II chords of D Phrygian Major. This is the only section where the second chord of the progression is placed on the downbeat 3 instead of beat 4. Also, the 5th to root resolution in the bass is abandoned in favor of a sustained D, the root of D Phrygian Major. The combined result emphasizes the tonality of D Phrygian Major and plays into the flamenco sound that it creates. Miles solos in D Phrygian, the scale that is used over phrygian major. His repetitive emphasis on the root (D), 2nd (Eb), and 3rd (F) gives more of the flamenco character to this section and provides somewhat of a motif.

Example 98: Bars 21 through 24 of "Flamenco Sketches."

This progression modulates to G Minor. The G Tonic Minor scale is used in this section, which supports both the V7 and Im7 chords that are used in this progression. Miles alludes to the G Tonic Minor scale as the scale choice for this section with the Am7 arpeggio (which is diatonic to G Tonic Minor), but it is Coltrane's solo that follows that clearly states G Tonic Minor as the scale used.

After Kind of Blue *was recorded Miles' great quintet and sextet of the late '50s gradually disbanded. Bill Evans had technically already left the group and was making some outstanding recordings with his trio that included Scott La Faro and Paul Motion. Cannonball Adderly went on to achieve great success with his own band as well. Miles managed to hold onto John Coltrane for a while longer. But even Coltrane was leading his own groups as a greater outlet for his own style and compositions. His groundbreaking album* Giant Steps *was recorded only two weeks after* Kind of Blue *was completed, a testament to Coltrane's overwhelming talent. He so poignantly soloed over the sparse chords on* Kind of Blue, *and showed his technical command of his instrument and the jazz language over the dense chords on* Giant Steps. *In March of 1961, Coltrane made his last recording as a member of Miles' band on the album* Some Day My Prince Will Come.

PFRANCING
(No Blues)
From the recording *Some Day My Prince Will Come* (Miles Davis)

By Miles Davis

Copyright © 1959 Jazz Horn Music
Copyright Renewed
All Rights Administered by Sony/ATV Music Publishing, 8 Music Square West, Nashville, TN 37203
International Copyright Secured   All Rights Reserved

PFRANCING

KEY: F Major
FORM: Blues

F7 I F Mix				

Bb7 IV Bb Mix		F7 I F Mix		

| Db7
bVI7
Db Mix#4 | C7#9
V | F7
I
F Mix | | |

"Pfrancing" is another basic blues by Miles. The only chord added to the basic structure is the D♭7 chord (♭VI7) in bar 9. The ♭VI7 chord followed by the V chord is common in jazz blues progressions. The ♭VI7 pushes downward to the V chord and the tension of the V chord resolves to the I chord. While the pull to the V chord is the specific function of the ♭VI7 chord, conveniently it is also the minor 3rd substitute for the IV chord, adding a little more relevance to the key.

Example 99: "Pfrancing."

The melody for "Pfrancing" is set up like "Blues by Five," with one motif and an ending. The main motif in the pick-up bar and bar 1 uses the F Blues scale (F A♭ B♭ C E♭) with the addition of the ♭5 (a common "blue" note). The motif ends on the root of the chord played underneath. As the chords change in bar 4 to B♭7, the motif is varied to fit over B♭7, yet still uses the F Blues scale. The B♭7 motif is repeated in bar 9 over D♭7 (the minor 3rd substitute for B♭7). Bars 9 through 12 end the melody with a blues statement derived from the F Blues scale.

By 1963, Miles was in search of a new quintet that would embody the brilliance of his '50s quintet. In the spring of 1963, he began to fulfill that goal. Miles recorded the album Seven Steps to Heaven *with two different bands. The album partly grew out of a collaboration with Victor Feldman, a well-known studio musician at the time. Miles and Feldman co-wrote the song "Seven Steps to Heaven" and Feldman wrote the song "Joshua." In April, a band consisting of Miles (trumpet), George Coleman (tenor sax), Victor Feldman (piano), Ron Carter (bass), and Frank Butler (drums), recorded four songs for the album in Los Angeles. In May, Miles recorded three more songs in New York with George Coleman (tenor sax), Herbie Hancock (piano), Ron Carter (bass), and Tony Williams (drums). The New York band would become Miles' working quintet over the next year. The introduction of Tony Williams into the band proved to be one of the most important elements of Miles' music through the end of the decade. Only seventeen at the time, Williams was already reshaping the art of jazz drumming. His technical brilliance, independence, and rhythmic command all became trademarks of jazz drumming in the years to follow. Ron Carter and Herbie Hancock also continued to work with Miles for the bulk of the '60s and greatly impacted the approach to jazz bass and piano as Williams did with drums. Carter and Hancock's ability to adapt to any song or playing situation was equally impressive to their individual talents on their instruments. Their presence became an unmistakable part of Miles' music and sound, and played an integral part in the songs instead of mere accompaniment.*

George Coleman, on the other hand, spent a little more than a year as part of Miles' working band. His contribution was no less significant than the other members, and his role with Miles would end more for Miles search for a new sound than Coleman's lack of talent. Apart from Coleman's playing of Seven Steps to Heaven, *he would play at the now well-known concert date at Carnegie Hall that yielded the albums* My Funny Valentine *and* Four & More *(now reissued as* The Complete Concert 1964*).*

SEVEN STEPS TO HEAVEN

From the recording *Seven Steps to Heaven* (Miles Davis), *The Complete Concert 1964 (My Funny Valentine + Four & More)* (Miles Davis)

By Miles Davis and Victor Feldman

SEVEN STEPS TO HEAVEN

KEY: F Major
FORM: AABA

Fmaj7	Bb7	Em7b5	A7	Dm7	Ab7	G7
I	IV7	II	V	I / VI	bIII7	II7
	Bb Mix#4	D HM			Ab Mix#4	G Mix

				Eb6	E6	F6
				bVIImaj7	VIImaj7	I
				Eb Lydian	E Major	

Fmaj7	Bb7	Em7b5	A7	Dm7	Ab7	G7
I	IV7	II	V	I / VI	bIII7	II7
	Bb Mix#4	D HM			Ab Mix#4	G Mix

				Eb6	E6	F6
				bVIImaj7	VIImaj7	I
				Eb Lydian	E Major	

Cmaj7		Dm7	G7	Em7		Fm7	Bb7
I		II	V	III		II	V
C Major						Eb Major	

Ebmaj7		Abm7	Db7	Gbmaj7		Gm7	C7
I		II	V	I		II	V
		Gb Major					

Fmaj7	Bbmaj7	Em7b5	A7	Dm7	Ab7	G7
I	IV7	II	V	I / VI	bIII7	II7
	Bb Mix#4	D HM		Ab Mix#4	G Mix	

				Eb6	E6	F6
				bVIImaj7	VIImaj7	I
				Eb Lydian	E Major	

Example 100: Intro and bridge for "Seven Steps to Heaven."

The intro to "Seven Steps to Heaven" uses a I7 chord, giving it a blues feel, to a ♭VII7 chord (minor 3rd substitute for the V chord). The melody is a repetitive phrase, using the 5th of the main key (F Major).

Example 101: Section A of "Seven Steps to Heaven."

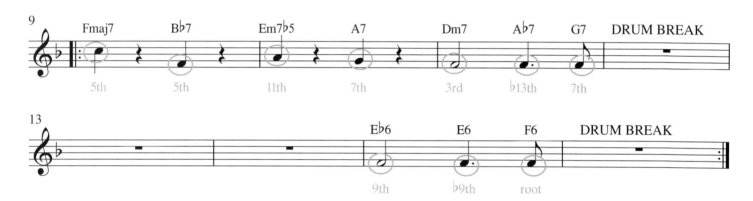

The melody for the A section is sparse and rhythmically reminiscent of "Miles." The entire A theme is in the main key of F Major, while the chords underneath are more diverse. A B♭7 chord is used in bar 9, again adding a blues element that was addressed in the introduction. A modulation to the relative minor (D Minor) is established in bar 10. The Em7♭5 functions as the VII chord in F Major and the II chord in D Minor. Similarly, bar 11 resolves the D Minor modulation to the I chord (Dm7), which splits its function as the VI chord in F Major. The ♭III7 chord creates downward pressure to the II chord, like a ♭VI7 → V progression in the blues. A chromatic line is created between the 5th of Dm7 (A♮), the root of A♭7 (A♭), and the root of G7 (G♮). In bar 15, a resolution to the I chord is set up using the ♭VIImaj7 and the VIImaj7 chords. In the song "Nardis" (see page 108), Miles used a ♭IImaj7 chord in place of the ♭II7 chord (the tritone substitute for the V chord). Both the root resolution and the complete chromaticism of a ♭IImaj7 to a Imaj7 provided resolution and added color to the ♭II chord. As jazz writing evolved into the '60s, this became a common application for not only the ♭II chord, but the ♭VII and VII chords as well. The ♭VII chord is the minor 3rd substitute for the V chord (in bar 7 this is an E♭ chord in place of a C chord). The original four-part species for these chords were E♭7 substituting for C7. When the chord species is changed, the resolution is still felt while the maj7 (E♭maj7) provides color. The VII chord was also used to resolve

I chord because of the tone behavior of the roots (see page 24). The seventh note of a key has a natural pull to the octave, providing resolution. Because of this, the root of a VII chord also provides resolution to the root of a I chord. It is common to find the species of the VII chord as either a 7th (VII7) or a maj7 (VIImaj7). The use of the ♭VIImaj7 and VIImaj7 in bar 15 provides anticipation for the resolutional I chord in bar 16, and creates complete chromatic movement between the chord tones.

Example 102:

E♭maj7 (♭VIImaj7)		Emaj7 (VIImaj7)		Fmaj7 (I)
E♭	→	E	→	F
G	→	G♯	→	A
B♭	→	B	→	C
D	→	D♯	→	E

Example 103: B section of "Seven Steps to Heaven."

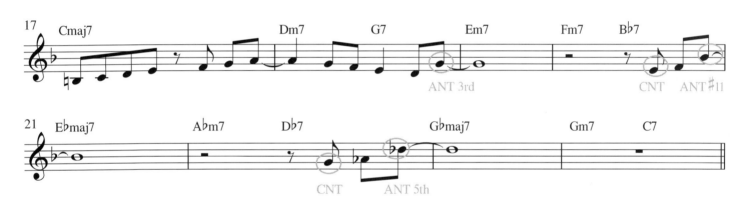

The song modulates from F Major to the key of the V chord (C Major) in bars 17 through 19. Then, the Em7 moves chromatically to Fm7 which begins a modulation to E♭ Major. The A♭m7 acts as an interchange for A♭maj7, the IV chord in E♭ Major. The A♭m7 begins another modulation to G♭ Major. The root of G♭maj7 in bar 23 moves up chromatically to the root of Gm7, which brings the song back to the main key of F Major. The rising melody in the B section makes use of a parallel phrase in bars 2/3, 4/5, and 6/7 to establish the B-section theme.

In September of 1964, the addition of Wayne Shorter to the quintet, replacing George Coleman on tenor saxophone, would complete the lineup for Miles' next great quintet. Shorter was already a significant voice in jazz with his work in Art Blakey's Jazz Messengers. Shorter at once rounded out the sound and vision of the quintet, and added some of the compositional style and solo voice that would define the band. Shorter had contributed heavily to the list of original songs played by the Jazz Messengers, and continued the same as part of Miles' quintet. Miles' records of the past had always used songs that were either Miles' originals or jazz standards. In contrast, the new recordings were entirely the result of originals by any one of the band members.

With the rising popularity of free jazz, improvised songs with no preset chord progression, and the still advancing language of the jazz soloist (partly due to Coltrane's work), the new quintet would have an immense amount of ideas and freedom within which to work. Many of Wayne Shorter's songs involved complicated chord progressions which often only implied keys rather than stated them. As unusual and unique as the songs became, the band always seemed to have the uncanny ability to evoke beauty and passion out of the music, where most players would be hard-pressed to navigate the chords.

In January of 1965, Miles completed his first studio recording (E.S.P.) with his new quintet. The album consisted of originals by each band member (or collaborations) with the exception of Tony Williams, who would contribute songs to later albums.

E.S.P.

From the recording *E.S.P.* (Miles Davis)

By Wayne Shorter

Copyright © 1965 MIYAKO MUSIC
Copyright Renewed
All Rights Administered by IRVING MUSIC, INC.
All Rights Reserved   Used by Permission

E.S.P.

KEY: F Major
FORM: 16 Bars

E7 VII7 E Mix♭2(♭6)		Fmaj7 I	

E7 VII7 E Mix♭2(♭6)		E♭maj7♯11 ♭VIImaj7 E♭ Lydian	

cycle asc. minor 2nd

D7 D Mix	E♭7♯11 E♭ Mix	E7♯9 / VII7 E Mix	Fmaj7 E♭7 I ♭VII7 E♭ Mix♯4

1.
Dm7 VI	G7 II7 G Mix	Gm7 II	G♭7 ♭II7 G♭ Mix

2.
D♭7♯11 ♭VI7 D♭ Mix♯4	C7 V	D♭7 G♭7 ♭VI7 ♭II7 D♭ Mix G♭ Mix♯4	F7 I7 F Mix

Example 104: The melody of "E.S.P."

The melody for "E.S.P." is very thematic, making use of both melodic and rhythmic repetition. The melody in bars 1 through 6 is constructed using all fourth intervals, referencing the very popular use of quartal chords in this era. The melody also ends with the use of fourth intervals in bars 19 and 20. The melody in bars 9 through 13 is identifiable through parallel rhythms. Bars 14 and 15 mimic the rhythms of the first motif, anticipating the return. The entire melody is made up of a series of arpeggios. Using the arpeggios from the melody as chords, a chord progression in F Major can be created.

PART II | THE COMPOSITIONS

Example 105: Chord progression created from the arpeggios in "E.S.P."

KEY: F Major

| Dm7 | | | | |
| VI | | | | |

| | | Fmaj7 | | |
| | | I | | |

| Dm7 | | Em7♭5 | | |
| VI | | VII | | |

1.
G7				
II7				
G Mix				

2.
E♭maj7			Dm7	
♭VIImaj7			VI	
E♭ Lydian				
(♭IImaj7 in D Minor)			(I in D Minor / VI)	

If you compare the functions of these chords with the functions of the chords actually used under the melody (see the analysis sheet on page 133), you will see many similarities. However, with the exception of the G7 arpeggio, none of the arpeggios are matched by the same chord underneath it.

Example 106: "E.S.P."

The first element of this chord progression that is readily apparent is the chromaticism. Connecting either roots of the chords or chord tones, a chromatic line is apparent throughout the chord progression.

Example 107:

$$E \to F \to E \to E\flat \to D \to E\flat \to E \to F/E \to E\flat \to$$

$$D \to D \to D \to D\flat \to (E)$$

$$D\flat \to C \to D\flat \to D\flat \to E$$

Since most of these chords are the same species and a half step away, entire chord progressions are moved chromatically. Example 107 is one way of viewing the chromaticism between the chords, as other lines can be derived as well.

The second readily apparent element of the chord progression is the extensive use of chromatic and partial diatonic chords. The following example is an exercise to understand a more direct function of these chords to the main key (F Major).

Using four of the chromatic and partial diatonic chords from "E.S.P." (E7, E♭7, D♭7, G♭7), this chart shows the minor 3rd substitutes for each chord.

E7	→	G7	→	B♭7	→	D♭7
E♭7	→	G♭7	→	A7	→	C7
D♭7	→	E7	→	G7	→	B♭7
G♭7	→	A7	→	C7	→	E♭7

Using these minor 3rd substitutes for the original chords, a chord progression more closely related to F Major can be created.

Example 108:

KEY: F Major

G7 II7 G Mix		Fmaj7 I		
G7 II7 G Mix		C7 V		

| F7
I7
F Mix | C7
V | G7
II7
G Mix | Fmaj75
I | C7
V |

1.
Dm7 VI	G7 II7 G Mix	Gm7 II	C7 V

2.
| G7
II7
G Mix | C7
V | G7   C7
II7   V
G Mix | F7
I7
F Mix |

Now, comparing the analysis sheet in example 108 with the original analysis sheet (page 133) you can see the chords in a more direct relationship to F Major. The melody, as well, is almost entirely in F Major. The arpeggios outside of F Major are still closely related with only two notes chromatic to the key: B♮ and E♭.

Without being present at the time Miles and Wayne Shorter wrote "E.S.P.", it is difficult to say decisively how they assembled the chord progression. However, through the analysis we are able to understand several ways in which "E.S.P." could have been developed.

1. It was more common in this era to use the melody note as an upper partial or alteration of the chord played underneath, instead of a chord tone. This is true of many of the chords against the melody in "E.S.P."

2. The arpeggios in the melody generated several chords which are used in the chord progression.

3. The chords of "E.S.P." create a chromatic line underneath the melody.

4. The use of minor 3rd substitution was commonly used in this era, and certainly can be seen in Miles' songs that have previously been discussed.

5. Wayne Shorter's writing style during this time typically used chords in a way that made the key more ambiguous. Coupled with the use of fourths in the melody, the chord progression in "E.S.P." certainly alludes to F Major more than directly stating it.

EIGHTY ONE

From the recording *E.S.P.* (Miles Davis)

By Miles Davis and Ronald Carter

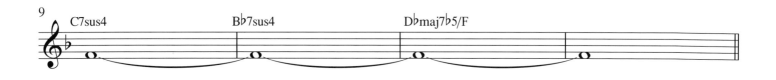

Copyright © 1965 Jazz Horn Music and Retrac Productions, Inc.
Copyright Renewed
All Rights on behalf of Jazz Horn Music Administered by
Sony/ATV Music Publishing, 8 Music Square West, Nashville, TN 37203
International Copyright Secured All Rights Reserved

EIGHTY ONE

KEY: F Major
FORM: 24 Bars

F7sus4 I F Mix			
B♭7sus4 IV B♭ Mix		F7sus4 I F Mix	
C7sus4 V	B♭7sus4 IV B♭ Mix	D♭maj7♭5/F ♭VImaj7 D♭ Lydian	
F7sus4 I F Mix	B♭7sus4 IV B♭ Mix	F7sus4 I F Mix	
B♭7sus4 IV B♭ Mix		F7sus4 I F Mix	
C7sus4 V	B♭7sus4 IV B♭ Mix	F7sus4 I F Mix	

"Eighty One" is constructed of two 12-bar sections. Each 12-bar section is based on a basic blues. Both sections add a IV chord (B♭7) in bar 10, a common addition to a basic blues. Similarly, a IV chord is added to bar 14, in the second section. The only unusual chord to a blues is the D♭maj7♭5 in the first section, which replaces the I chord. This chord adds some color to the progression, while still alluding to the F7 (I chord) with an F in the bass. Many of the chords in "Eighty One" are voiced as quartal chords (see page 17). Anytime you see a sus4, 11, or m11 chord during this era, there is a good chance some quartal voicing is being used.

Example 109: Quartal chords created from voicing a chord with all perfect or augmented 4th intervals.

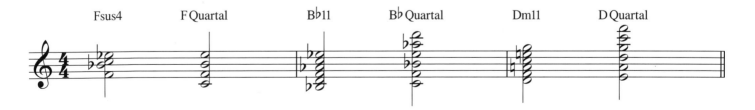

Example 110: Bars 1 through 4 of "Eighty One."

The melody in bars 1 and 2 basically outlines the F7 chord played underneath with the use of a ♭13 (D♭) as a color tone. In bars 3 and 4, a quick six-note phrase is used. Four of the notes reference F7 (F and E♭), while two alterations for the chord are added (G♭ and D♭). There are two ways to perceive the origin of this phrase:

1. The G♭ and D♭ notes function as the ♭9 and ♭13 of F7. Both are acceptable alterations to use over a 7th chord (see page 16).

2. John Coltrane's use of chord substitution and subsequent scale substitution had an enormous impact on jazz soloing and composition. When Coltrane approached a 7th chord, F7, for example, through minor 3rd substitution, he viewed the chord as either F7, A♭7, C♭7, or D7. The typical scales used over these chords are F Mixolydian, A♭ Mixolydian, C♭ Mixolydian, and D Mixolydian respectively. So, when Coltrane played over an F7 chord, he was just as likely to use F Mixolydian as he was A♭ Mixolydian, C♭ Mixolydian, or D Mixolydian because of minor 3rd substitution. In bar 4 of "Eighty One," the six notes of the melody are strongly indicative of an A♭ Mixolydian scale: A♭ B♭ C D♭ E♭ F G♭. The presence of A♭ Mixolydian in the melody certainly reinforces both the D♭ note in bar 2, and the use of the D♭maj7 chord in bar 10 (D♭maj7 is the IV chord of A♭ Mixolydian).

Example 111: Bars 13 through 16 of "Eighty One."

Bar 13 begins the second 12-bar blues of the song. Instead of reusing the melody in bars 1 through 4, a new melody is created. The notes of bars 13 and 14 arpeggiate a B♭7 chord, which is supported by the addition of the B♭7 in bar 14.

Example 112: Bars 5 through 12 of "Eighty One."

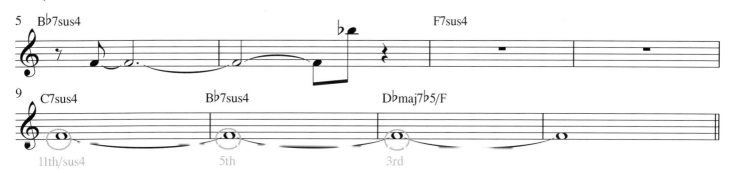

Example 113: Bars 17 through 24 of "Eighty One."

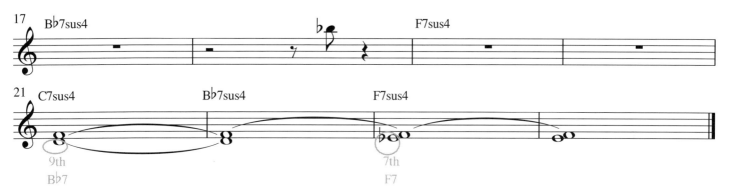

These two sections make use of basically the same melody. The sustained F note in bars 5 and 6 is omitted, while maintaining the ear-catching B♭ note on the upbeat of 3. The sustained F note in bars 9 through 12 both threads together the chords played underneath and provides resolution to the root of the key. The sustained F note is repeated in bars 21 through 24, this time adding a second melody which implies a IV to I resolution (B♭7 to F7).

Miles in the Sky was the fifth studio release of Miles' '60s quintet, following *E.S.P., Miles Smiles, Sorcerer,* and *Nefertiti. The album is perhaps Miles' first push toward fusion that would be fully realized on* Bitches Brew. Miles in the Sky *included some electric piano work by Herbie Hancock and added guitarist George Benson to one track ("Paraphernalia").*

"STUFF"

The chords for "Stuff" make extensive use of minor 3rd substitution, much as "E.S.P." had. "Stuff" is in the key of D♭ Major. The minor 3rd substitutes for the I7, IV7, and V are as follows:

D♭7 (I7) → E7 → G7 → B♭7

G♭7 (IV7) → A7 → C7 → E♭7

A♭7 (V) → B7 → D7 → F7

Using minor 3rd substitution, every chord in "Stuff" can be converted to a I7, IV7 or V chord.

Example 114: Alternate chords for "Stuff" using the minor 3rd substitutes.

KEY: D♭ Major

D♭7 I7		A♭7 V		
D♭7 I7		G♭7 IV7		
D♭7 I7		G♭7 IV7		
D♭maj7 I				
A♭7 V				
A♭7 V				
D♭7 I7		(D♭7)		
		A♭7 V	D♭7 I7	
G♭7 IV7	D♭7 I7	(D♭7)		
(D♭7)				
(D♭7)			(D♭7)	

The use of minor 3rd substitution has been a recurring principle in Miles' writing style. It is important to understand minor 3rd substitution not as a random substitution for variety, but as careful construction of a chord progression and support of a melody. Notice on the original analysis sheet (page 147) that the chords audibly create a modulation to B♭ Major. Without the use of D♭maj7 in bars 13 through 16 and the Cm7/F in bars 21 through 24, "Stuff" may just as well be perceived as being in the key of D♭ Major, E Major, G Major, or B♭ Major through minor 3rd substitution. Even the modulation to B♭ Major can be reduced to the I7, IV7, and V chords in B♭ Major.

Example 115: Chords of bars 21 through 34 using minor 3rd substitution.

KEY OF MODULATION: B♭ Major

| F7 | | | | |
| V | | | | |

| B♭7 | | (B♭7) | | |
| I7 | | | | |

| | | F7 | B♭7 | |
| | | V | I7 | |

| C7 | B♭7 | | | |
| II7 | I7 | | | |

What we *are* left with, however, are the chords on the original analysis sheet which function in the key of D♭ Major with one modulation to B♭ Major. The ambiguity of the key that the chord progression creates and the extensive use of 7th chords (which allows the most freedom in terms of alterations and scales) gives "Stuff" the progressive sound that Miles' '60s quintet was known for.

STUFF

From the recording *Miles in the Sky* (Miles Davis)

By Miles Davis

STUFF

KEY: D♭ Major
FORM: 45 Bars

D♭7#9 I7 D♭ Mix		C♭7 ♭VII7 C♭ Mix#4	
B♭7 VI7 B♭ Mix#4		C7 VII7 C Mix	
B♭7 VI7 B♭ Mix#4		C7#5(#9) VII7 C Mix	
D♭/C I			
A♭7 V			
Cm7/F V B♭ Major			
E7#11 #IV7 E Mix#4		B♭7 I7 B♭ Mix	
		A♭7 ♭VII7 A♭ Mix#4	G7 VI7 G Mix
C7 II7 C Mix♭2(♭6)	B♭7 I7 B♭ Mix	G7#5 #IV7 G Mix♭2(♭6)	
D♭7#9 II7 D♭ Mix			

The melody for "Stuff" seems to have been written after the chord progression. The melody follows the chords with either chord tones or notes from the appropriate scale. The melody is constructed of short melodic phrases that all relate to each other through rhythmic repetition.

Example 116: Bars 1 through 4 of "Stuff."

Example 117: Bars 13 through 16 of "Stuff."

Example 118: Bars 27 through 30 of "Stuff."

The short phrases are even more distinguished as the head is repeated several times. Melodic phrases that begin on beat 3 the first time are on beat 1 the second time; whole notes become half notes; etc. The loose feel of the song and the interrelationship of all of the chords allow the melodic phrases to be moved around without destroying the integrity of the song.

PART II | THE COMPOSITIONS

IT'S ABOUT THAT TIME

From the recording *In a Silent Way* (Miles Davis)

By Miles Davis

Copyright © 1970 Jazz Horn Music
Copyright Renewed
All Rights Administered by Sony/ATV Music Publishing, 8 Music Square West, Nashville, TN 37203
International Copyright Secured   All Rights Reserved

IT'S ABOUT THAT TIME

KEY: F Mixolydian
FORM: Extended Vamp

F7#9
I
F Mixolydian

VAMP FOR LENGTH OF SONG

149

Following Miles in the Sky *were two more fusion-oriented albums:* Filles de Kilamanjaro *and* In a Silent Way. *Both of these albums drastically shifted the focus of Miles' music and unmistakably were the path to his landmark recordings for* Bitches Brew. *Unlike the songs of the quintet's albums, the songs of* Filles de Kilamanjaro *and* In a Silent Way *were exclusively written by Miles, with the exception of the song "In a Silent Way" by Joe Zawinul. The elements of the songs are the same elements of the songs on* Bitches Brew. *Miles again embraced modality in the songs, while the soloist's and the accompanist's language was much freer. The rhythms were loose and gravitated toward rock and funk using either straight or swing eighths. The overall mood of the music seemed to dictate the course of the song above all else.*

For two of the songs on Filles de Kilamanjaro, *Miles replaced Herbie Hancock and Ron Carter with Chick Corea and Dave Holland, two names which became an important part of Miles' fusion movement. On the album* In a Silent Way, *Miles began to add more players to the band to diversify the sound. The players on* In a Silent Way *are as follows: Miles Davis (trumpet), Herbie Hancock (electric piano), Chick Corea (electric piano), Joe Zawinul (electric piano and organ), Wayne Shorter (tenor sax), John McLaughlin (guitar), Dave Holland (bass), and Tony Williams (drums). The astounding part of the album was that with eight players instead of five, Miles managed to get more space in the music and deliver very striking pieces in terms of mood and presence.*

During this period, most of Miles' songs were based on one chord or one mode, usually the mixolydian mode. By using the mixolydian mode, Miles found an intense amount of harmonic, melodic, and rhythmic freedom in the music. Writing a song in F Mixolydian as "It's About That Time" is, gives a reference point for the entire band. Both the accompanist and soloist have a starting point and framework within the F Mixolydian scale: F G A B♭ C D E♭. The accompanist can readily use F7, Cm7, and E♭maj7 as much as Fm11, Cm9, or E♭maj13. Looking back at page 16, you'll notice that of all of the chord species, a 7th chord accepts the most upper partials and alterations (eleven out of twelve notes in a a chromatic scale). So, it is not unlikely to find the players adding some of those alterations or upper partials to the chords or solo. The F7 can now be thought of as F7♯9, F13♯11, F9♭5, etc. Using the minor 3rd substitution principle, the F7 can also be thought of as A♭7, C♭7, and D7, each bearing their relative scales, upper partials, and alterations. It is because of all of these possibilities over or in place of a 7th chord that Miles' music from this period sounded so diverse, and yet still referenced the main chord and tonality.

PART II | THE COMPOSITIONS

Example 119: "It's About That Time."

As you can see in example 119, Miles used several alterations for an F7 chord in the melody of "It's About That Time." Notice how most of the melody uses chord tones from F7 (F A C E♭) and adds the alterations to color and contrast the melody.

Miles' rhythmic feel in his solos was always loose, playing ahead or behind the beat at his discretion. With songs like "It's About That Time" with only one chord, there are no chord changes to follow. So, all of the the band members can play freely over the chord without having to be concerned with keeping time, only tempo. This added rhythmic freedom is evident in both the comping and the soloing. This comes fully into focus on *Bitches Brew*, with intense polyrhythmic interaction of the band.

In August of 1969, Miles recorded the extremely successful double album Bitches Brew. *The music embraced the advanced language of jazz within a rock/funk setting.* Bitches Brew *seemed to bring together everything Miles had been experimenting with before. The songs were filled with dense rhythmic interplay as there were twelve or more players on each track. The songs were equally dense with music and yet never seemed crowded or filled with harmonic clashes. In Bitches Brew, Miles was responding and becoming part of the rock music that dominated the music market and social climate of the late '60s. While Miles was heavily criticized at the time for abandoning jazz, his work on* Bitches Brew *is nonetheless astonishing and paved the way for fusion.* Bitches Brew *gave Miles his first gold album, and excerpts from the songs on the album (as most were ten to twenty minutes) even found their way to the radio airwaves that were only playing rock. Miles' success with the album allowed him immense exposure and gave him opportunities to play concerts along with major rock bands of the time. While Miles' music perhaps turned its back on the jazz he had so much been a part of, Miles certainly had always embraced and defined the music of the time which* Bitches Brew *so eloquently delivered.*

PART II | THE COMPOSITIONS

MILES RUNS THE VOODOO DOWN

From the recording *Bitches Brew* (Miles Davis)

By Miles Davis

Copyright © 1969 Jazz Horn Music
Copyright Renewed
All Rights Administered by Sony/ATV Music Publishing, 8 Music Square West, Nashville, TN 37203
International Copyright Secured   All Rights Reserved

MILES RUNS THE VOODOO DOWN

KEY: F Mixolydian
FORM: Extended Vamp

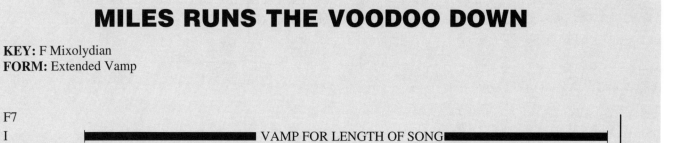

"Miles Runs the Voodoo Down" continues Miles' writing style used on *Filles de Kilamanjaro* and *In a Silent Way*. The F7 chord functions exactly the same as in "It's About That Time" (see page 150 for a review of its usage).

Example 120: "Miles Runs the Voodoo Down."

Miles uses a ♯9 in the melody much as he had in "It's About That Time." The ♯9 functions the same as the ♭3 of the blues scale. The use of "blue" notes throughout *Bitches Brew* is a natural complement to the rock/funk rhythms that dominate the album.

PART III
Miles Davis: The Player

Part III focuses on Miles Davis the soloist. The section that follows is an overview of the typical elements of a jazz solo. These principles or devices are elements you would expect to find in any jazz solo. For example, the review of scales will help you understand why the scales on the analysis sheets are considered the basic scale choice. As Miles' solos are reviewed, the basic scales indicate what you would expect Miles to use. Then, you can concentrate strictly on how Miles uses the scale or why he deviated from the scale. The goal of the solo analysis is for you to understand Miles' usage and application of theoretical principles. This will help you realize how a jazz solo is developed and give you a feel for Miles' unique voice in this idiom. Once you have read Part III and processed the information on soloing, a review of Part I will be useful, as the construction of a jazz melody uses elements of a jazz solo.

SCALES

There are fourteen basic scales that are used on the analysis sheets. These scales represent the maximum number of scales needed to play through any chord progression. As you will find in reviewing Miles' solos, these scales also represent the typical scale choices for a jazz soloist. Unless a soloist is using scale substitution, you will find most jazz solos are played through exclusively using these scales. Deviations from the scale are often easily explained through the principles on **arpeggios** or **melodic devices** (such as alterations or chromatic passing tones). The fourteen basic scales, including their abbreviations, are:

Major	Natural Minor (NM)	Whole Tone
Lydian	Harmonic Minor (HM)	Diminished
Mixolydian (Mix)	Tonic Minor (TM)	Locrian
Mixolydian ♯4 (Mix♯4)	Dorian	
Mixolydian ♭2(♭6) (Mix♭2(♭6))	Phrygian	
	Aeolian	

BASIC SCALE FORMULAS

Major scale—The major scale is built from a series of whole steps (major 2nd intervals) and half steps (minor 2nd intervals).

　　　　Formula:　　W　W　1/2　W　W　W　1/2
　　　　F major:　　F　G　A　B♭　C　D　E

All of the other scales are created from altering the major scale. The following four scales are related to the major scale because they all contain a major I chord.

Lydian (♯4)
Example: F Major: 　F　G　A　B♭　C　D　E
　　　　　F Lydian: 　F　G　A　B　C　D　E

Mixolydian (♭7)
　　　F Mixolydian (F Mix): F　G　A　B♭　C　D　E♭

Mixolydian ♯4 (♯4, ♭7)
　　　F Mixolydian ♯4 (F Mix♯4): F　G　A　B　C　D　E♭

Mixolydian ♭2(♭6) (♭2, ♭6, ♭7)
　　　F Mixolydian ♭2(♭6) (F Mix♭2(♭6)):　F　G♭　A　B♭　C　D♭　E♭

Similarly, all of the following scales are related to the natural minor scale because they all have a minor I chord.

Natural Minor (♭3, ♭6, ♭7)
　　　F Natural Minor (NM): F　G　A♭　B♭　C　D♭　E♭

Harmonic Minor (♭3, ♭6)
　　　F Harmonic Minor (HM):　F　G　A♭　B♭　C　D♭　E

Tonic Minor (♭3)
　　　F Tonic Minor (TM):　F　G　A♭　B♭　C　D　E

Dorian (♭3, ♭7)

    F Dorian: F G A♭ B♭ C D E♭

Phrygian (♭2, ♭3, ♭6, ♭7)

    F Phrygian: F G♭ A♭ B♭ C D♭ E♭

Aeolian (♭3, ♭6, ♭7—same spelling as natural minor)

    F Aeolian: F G A♭ B♭ C D♭ E♭

The locrian scale is distinguished from the other scales because its I chord is diminished.

Locrian (♭2, ♭3, ♭5, ♭6, ♭7)

    F Locrian: F G♭ A♭ B♭ C♭ D♭ E♭

Both the diminished and the whole tone scales are unique because of their symmetric intervals. A diminished scale is built from a series of repeated whole and half steps.

F Diminished: F   G   A♭   B♭   C♭   D♭   E♭♭   F♭
                          W   1/2   W   1/2   W   1/2   W

The whole tone scale is built from a series of whole steps:

F Whole Tone: F   G   A   B   C♯   D♯
                           W   W   W   W   W

SCALE ANALYSIS

Each scale listed on the analysis sheet is based on three specific factors:

1. The chord.

2. The following chord.

3. The key or modal tonality.

Each scale is selected for a chord from either a horizontal or vertical solution. Horizontal solutions are those in which the root of the scale is also the root of the key center. There are three main categories that fall under horizontal solutions.

1. **Full Diatonic**—The chord is part of the main key and will take the scale of the main key as the solution.

For example, on the analysis sheet the key or tonality that is written at the top left is the main key. If that key is F Major, then every chord that is part of the key (full diatonic) will take F Major as the scale solution.

F Major	Chord Function	Scale Solution
Fmaj7	I	F Major
Gm7	II	F Major
Am7	III	F Major
B♭maj7	IV	F Major
C7	V	F Major
Dm7	VI	F Major
Em7♭5	VII	F Major

On the analysis sheets, if no scale solution is written under a chord, the scale of the main key is used. This only applies to major keys and modes.

Example 121: Bars 1 through 4 of "Tune Up."

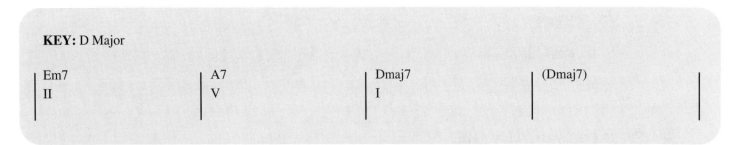

In the song "Tune Up," the main key is D Major. In bars 1 through 4 of the song, a II → V → I progression in D Major is established. Since Em7, A7, and Dmaj7 are all full diatonic to D Major, all three chords will take a D Major scale. D Major is not written under the chords, indicating the scale of the main key (D Major) is used.

2. **Internal Modulation**—If a new key is established, the chords of that key are bracketed together on the analysis sheet. The full-diatonic chords of the modulation will take the scale of the new key. For example, if the key of B♭ Major is established, the full-diatonic chords will take a B♭ Major scale.

Example 122: Bars 5 through 8 of "Tune Up."

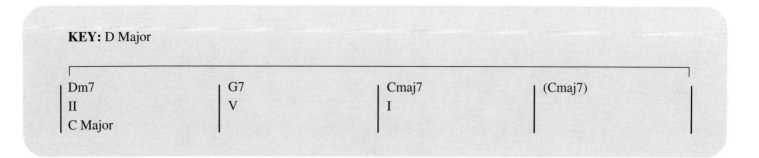

In bars 5 through 8 of "Tune Up," the song modulates from D Major to C Major. The modulation is bracketed and now every chord under that bracket that is full diatonic to C Major will take the C Major scale. The key of the modulation (C Major) is listed once, and then every full-diatonic chord under that bracket will take the same scale solution.

3. **Unresolved**—If a new key is entered, but does not use the resolutional I, VI, or III chord, the chords will still be solved by using the scale of the implied key.

Example 123: Bars 1 through 4 of "Four."

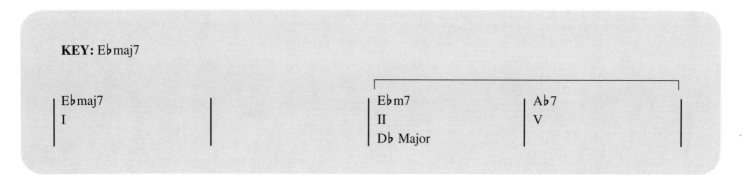

"Four" begins on the I chord (E♭maj7) of the main key (E♭ Major). Since there is no scale solution listed under the E♭maj7 chord, you know the scale of the main key (E♭ Major) should be used. In bars 3 and 4, a modulation to the D♭ Major is established. We know this modulation is unresolved because the active chords never resolve to a passive chord. The chords are still full diatonic to D♭ Major and take the scale of the implied key (D♭ Major scale). Again, the main scale is listed once and then every full-diatonic chord under the bracket will take that scale.

Vertical solutions are those in which the root of the scale will also be the root of the chord. Vertical scale solutions will always be a different scale than the main key or key of a modulation. There are three main groups for vertical solutions:

1. **Partial diatonic** chords are chords whose root is part of the key but species is not. The scale solution for these chords will have the same root as the chord.

Example 124: Bars 1 through 4 of "Little Willie Leaps."

KEY: F Major

Fmaj7	Gm7	C7	Am7	D7	Gm7	C7
I	II	V	III	VI7	II	V
				D Mix♭2(♭6)		

The D7 in bar 3 is a secondary dominant to the Gm7 in bar 4 (VI7 → II). The D7 is partial diatonic to the main key (F Major) because its root is part of the key, but its species is not (the full-diatonic chord to F Major with a D root is Dm7). The D7 chord then takes a scale that is named from the root of the chord (D).

2. **Chromatic** chords are chords whose roots are not diatonic to the key. The scale solution for these chords also is named from the root of the chord.

Example 125: Bars 17 through 20 of "Swing Spring."

KEY: B♭ Major

B♭m7	A7	A♭m7	G7
II	♭II7	II	♭II7
A♭ Major	A Mix♯4	G♭ Major	G Mix♯4

There are two unresolved modulations in this section of "Swing Spring." The first modulation is to the key of A♭ Major. Since the B♭m7 is the full-diatonic II chord of A♭ Major, the scale solution is A♭ Major. Similarly, the A♭m7 in bar 19 is the full-diatonic II chord of the next modulation to G♭ Major. Its scale solution is G♭ Major. The A7 in bar 18 and the G7 in bar 20 both function as a ♭II7 in their respective keys. They are examples of chromatic chords because their roots are not part of the implied keys. Therefore, the scale solution for these chords will be different from the key of the modulation and will take a vertical scale solution with the same root as the chromatic chord.

3. A **Cycle** is a group of chords related to each other by either equidistant interval, equidistant root interval, or identical species. The scale solution for the chords of a cycle are named from the root of the chord.

Example 126: Bars 11 through 14 of "Circle."

KEY: D Minor

root cycle asc. minor 2nd

Gmaj7	A♭maj7	A7	Fmaj7
I/		/V	III
G Major	A♭ Lydian	A Mix♭2(♭6)	D NM

The chords in bars 11 through 13 are part of a root cycle in which the roots ascend each time by a minor second interval. Chords of a cycle typically have no Roman numerals underneath them, because their only function is within the cycle and not part of a specific key. In the example above, the Gmaj7 has a split function as the I chord of the previous modulation and as the first chord of the cycle. The A7 in bar 13 also splits its function between a chord of the root cycle and the V chord of the main key, D Minor. Since the chords of a cycle do not have a relationship to a key and only to each other, the chords take a vertical scale solution in which the root of the scale is the root of the chord.

All vertical scale solutions are initially guided by the species of the chord. The fourteen basic scales are grouped together according to the species of each I chord's triad (see page 155). In the chart below, the scales are broken down further to identify those scales that not only fit over the triad of the I chord (major, minor, diminished, and augmented), but the four-part species as well.

Each four-part chord species has listed underneath it the possible scales that can be played over it.

VERTICAL SCALE SOLUTIONS

maj7	7	m7	m6
Major	Mixolydian	Dorian	Dorian
Lydian	Mixolydian ♯4	Aeolian	
	Mixolydian ♭2(♭6)	Phrygian	

m(maj7)	m7♭5(ø7)	dim7	+7
Harmonic Minor	Locrian	Diminished	Whole Tone
Tonic Minor			

(root of scale = root of chord)

The chord species with only one scale solution have only one common scale choice. On the other hand, the chord species with more than one solution have several basic scales that can fit over that chord. The "best" scale to use is chosen by examining both the chord you are on and the following chord. By doing this, the connection of the two chords is more fluid.

Using the example of the partial-diatonic chord, we will use the vertical scale chart to find a scale solution.

Example 127: Bars 1 through 4 of "Little Willie Leaps."

KEY: F Major

Fmaj7	Gm7 C7	Am7 D7	Gm7 C7
I	II V	III VI7	II V

We have established that the D7 is partial diatonic to the key of F Major and that D will be the root of the scale. Using the vertical scale solution chart, the basic scale choices are:

D Mix	D E F♯ G A B C
D Mix♯4	D E F♯ G♯ A B C
D Mix♭2(♭6)	D E♭ F♯ G A B♭ C

Examining the chord following D7, which is Gm7, will help determine the "best" scale choice. The notes of Gm7 are G B♭ D F. Of the three choices, only the Mix ♭2(♭6) has a B♭ which anticipates the Gm7 chord. The two other scales can be used, but for the purpose of remaining fluid from chord to chord, the D Mix ♭2(♭6) is the "best" choice.

Some of these scales have exactly the same notes in them but are called two different names. The D Mix ♭2(♭6) (D E♭ F♯ G A B♭ C) is identical to G Harmonic Minor (G A B♭ C D E♭ F♯). This helps explain why the Mix ♭2(♭6) is an excellent choice for the D7 chord. The D7 and Gm7 mimic a V → I resolution as if the two chords were in G Minor. The Mix♭2(♭6) scale is used here instead of the harmonic minor scale because the D7 is not a V chord in G Minor, it is a VI7 chord in F Major. The D Mix♭2(♭6) reaffirms the partial-diatonic function of the chord.

Re-examining the cycle will help further understand vertical scale solutions.

Example 128: Bars 11 through 14 of "Circle."

```
KEY: D Minor
                    root cycle asc. minor 2nd
| Gmaj7          | A♭maj7        | A7              | Fmaj7   |
| I/             |               |         /V      | III     |
| G Major        | A♭ Major      | A Mix♭2(♭6)     | D NM    |
```

Gmaj7 solution: The scale choices for the Gmaj7 chord are G Major and G Lydian. Although the C♯ of G Lydian would complement the A♭maj7 acting as the 4th or 11th (D♭), the C♮ in G Major is the chord-tone 3rd of A♭maj7, making the G Major scale directly anticipate the A♭maj7 and the better choice.

A♭maj7 solution: Similarly, the D♭ note in the A♭ Major scale directly anticipates the chord-tone 3rd of A7 (C♯ or enharmonically D♭).

A7 solution: The scale choices for a 7th chord again are Mix, Mix♯4, and Mix♭2(♭6).

A Mix	A B C♯ D E F♯ G
A Mix♯4	A B C D♯ E F♯ G
A Mix♭2(♭6)	A B♭ C♯ D E F G

Since A Mix ♭2(♭6) is the only scale that has an F♮ which anticipates the root of the following chord, Fmaj7, it is the "best" scale choice to play over the A7.

Note: Some of the vertical scale solutions are the scales of the modes. The use of these scales does not mean you have entered that mode, they are simply the altered scale that works over that chord (see page 12 for explanation).

THE SCALES FOR A MINOR KEY

In major keys, the major scale is used for all full-diatonic chords. In minor keys, however, the solutions become more diverse. To begin with, the chords in a minor key are derived from two scale sources, the natural minor scale and the harmonic minor scale.

Example 129: The A Natural Minor and A Harmonic Minor scales.

```
A NM      A  B  C  D  E  F  G
A HM      A  B  C  D  E  F  G♯
```

The natural minor scale is derived from a major scale by flatting the third, sixth, and seventh (♭3, ♭6, ♭7). In the natural minor scale the resolutional I chord is a m7 chord. However, in a natural minor scale, the powerful tension of a V7 chord is lost, since the V chord is a m7 chord. To remedy this problem, the harmonic minor scale is used to establish a V chord that is a 7th chord. Now there is one scale with a Im7 chord and another scale with a V7 chord. The rest of the minor-key chords are pulled from the two scales based on diatonic substitution (*passive* for *passive* and *active* for *active*). The natural minor scale provides the passive substitutes for the I chord: III and VI. The harmonic minor scale provides the active substitutes for the V chord: II, IV, and VII. The chord species for a minor key are then as follows:

Chord species of a minor key.

Chord Function	Chord Name	Shown in A Minor
I	m7	Am7
II	m7(♭5)	Bm7(♭5)
III	maj7	Cmaj7
IV	m7	Dm7
V	7	E7
VI	maj7	Fmaj7
VII	dim7	G♯dim7

Now to establish scale solutions in a minor key, two scales will be used.

1. The I, III, and VI chords of a minor key use the natural minor scale of the I chord.

2. The II, IV, V, and VII chords of a minor key use the harmonic minor scale of the I chord.

While the II and IV chords are active chords in a minor key, their unique status of taking either the natural or harmonic minor scale allows them some flexibility. It is not uncommon to find a soloist use the natural minor scale over the II or IV chords of a minor key. Many times the usage of the natural minor scale instead of the harmonic minor is determined by the chord preceding or following the II or IV chord. For example, in a minor blues (see page 38), the IV chord in bar 5 is placed in between two I chords. To create a fluid sound in a I → IV → I minor progression, the natural minor scale is used over the IV chord.

Note: Partial diatonic and chromatic chords used in minor keys take the same vertical scale solutions as they would in major keys.

MODES

When a song is written in a mode, the scale choice is the same name as the mode. For a song that is in D Dorian, the soloist would use a D Dorian scale. Don't confuse the scale groupings that were used for the vertical scale solutions as implying that there are interchangeable scales that can be used in a mode. There is only one scale choice in a mode, and any note outside the scale or substituted scale is utilizing more advanced techniques. The modes and their spellings are as follows:

Ionian (same spelling as major)
    C Ionian: C D E F G A B

Dorian (♭3, ♭7)
    C Dorian: C D E♭ F G A B♭

Phrygian (♭2, ♭3, ♭6, ♭7)
    C Phrygian: C D♭ E♭ F G A♭ B♭

Lydian (♯4)
    C Lydian: C D E F♯ G A B

Mixolydian (♭7)
    C Mixolydian: C D E F G A B♭

Aeolian (♭3, ♭6, ♭7–same spelling as natural minor)
    C Aeolian: C D E♭ F G A♭ B♭

Locrian (♭2, ♭3, ♭5, ♭6, ♭7)
    C Locrian: C D♭ E♭ F G♭ A♭ B♭

THE BLUES AND PENTATONIC SCALES

Although the blues and pentatonic scales are not used on the analysis sheets, they should be considered basic scales and part of a jazz player's vocabulary. The analysis sheets use a seven-note scale as the solution for a blues, allowing the extra flexibility needed to interpret a blues in the jazz style. Both the pentatonic and blues scales are made up of five notes. A pentatonic scale is a derivative of a major scale, using five notes directly from the major scale.

Pentatonic scale formula: R 2 3 5 6
F Pentatonic: F G A C D

The blues scale is a derivative of the natural minor scale, using five notes directly from the natural minor scale.

Blues scale formula: R ♭3 4 5 ♭7
F Blues: F A♭ B♭ C E♭

Although the pentatonic scale can only be used over a I chord that is major, the blues scale is diverse enough to handle both a minor and a major I chord. In a major blues, the I chord is typically a I7 chord. If the I chord were an F7, its spelling would be F A C E♭. The only note of an F Blues scale that contradicts the F7 chord is the A♭ note. However, A♭ is enharmonically G♯, which is the ♯9 of F7 and an acceptable alteration for a 7th chord. This allows the blues scale to work over both a major and minor I chord. Due to the usage of the blues scale, you will find a ♯9 notated as ♭3rd, which is why a ♭3rd is commonly referred to as a "blue" note.

The following two charts show which chords in a major or minor key can take the blues or pentatonic scales.

In a major key, the blues scale of the I chord will work over any of the following chord functions (the key of F Major is used in this example, so the F Blues scale is the blues scale of the I chord):

I7	II	II7	IV7	V	VI	VI7	♭VII7
F7	Gm7	G7	B♭7	C7	Dm7	D7	E♭7

In a minor key, the following chord functions can use the blues scale of the I chord (shown in F Minor using the F Blues scale):

I	II	II7	III	IV	IV7	V	VI	♭VII7
Fm7	Gm7♭5	G7	A♭maj7	B♭m7	B♭7	C7	D♭maj7	E♭7

The pentatonic scale with the same root as the I chord will work over any of the following chords in a major key (shown in F Major using F Pentatonic):

I	II	III	IV	V	VI	♭VII7	VII
Fmaj7	Gm7	Am7	B♭maj7	C7	Dm7	E♭7	Em7♭5
I6	II7	III7	IV6				
F6	G7	A7	B♭6				
I7							
F7							

A mixture of the blues and pentatonic scales can also be used. The combination of an F Blues and an F Pentatonic would be as follows:

F Blues: F   A♭   B♭   C   E♭
F Pentatonic: F   G   A   C   D

Combination of F Blues and Pentatonic:
F   G   A♭   A   B♭   C   D   E♭

When a soloist uses a mixture of the blues and pentatonic scales, it doesn't necessarily mean the full combination of the two scales is used. For example, a soloist may use the F pentatonic scale with the added ♭3rd: F   G   A♭ A   C   D.

Example 130: Second chorus of Miles' solo in "Vierd Blues."

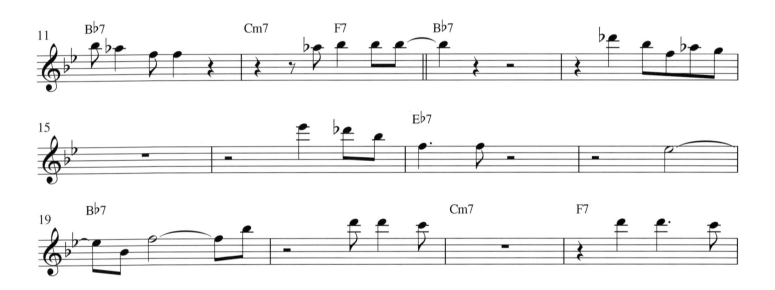

Miles predominantly uses the B♭ Blues scale over *all* of the chords of this blues. In bar 14, he adds a G note which is borrowed from the B♭ Pentatonic scale.

Below are two charts that display both a horizontal (root of scale = root of I chord) and vertical (root of scale = root of chord) approach. Each chart displays when the basic I, IV, and V chords of a blues can take either a **pentatonic scale, blues scale,** or **mixture** of the pentatonic and blues.

Horizontal (root of scale = root of I chord).

KEY: F Major **F7 (I7)**	**B♭7 (IV7)**	**C7 (V)**
F Blues	F Blues	F Blues
F Pentatonic		F Pentatonic
Mixture		Mixture

Vertical (root of scale = root of chord).

KEY: F Major **F7 (I7)**	**B♭7 (IV7)**	**C7 (V)**
F Blues	B♭ Blues	C Blues
F Pentatonic	B♭ Pentatonic	C Pentatonic
F Mixture	B♭ Mixture	C Mixture

ARPEGGIOS

Arpeggios are a large part of a jazz soloist's vocabulary. Most soloists use a four-part arpeggio; playing the root, third, fifth, and seventh of a chord.

Example 131: Four-part arpeggios.

Three-part arpeggios are used less frequently than four part, but are still common in jazz improvisation. A three-part arpeggio typically uses the root, third, and fifth of a chord. But, in some cases it states the third, fifth, and seventh of a chord.

Example 132: Three-part arpeggios.

The first two arpeggios directly state the root, third, and fifth of the chord they are played over. The next arpeggio states the third, fifth, and seventh of the chord (Gm7). Because of the arpeggio's close relationship to the chord it is played over, the arpeggio can be named from the chord it is played over (Gm7–knowing the root has been omitted), just as well it can be named from the root of the triad (B♭).

INVERSIONS

Arpeggios, much like chords, can be played in inversions. An inversion of an arpeggio begins the arpeggio on either the third, fifth, or seventh, instead of the root. The inverted arpeggio follows the same sequence of notes that is established in root position. In other words, the root is followed by the third, by the fifth, by the seventh, by the root, by the third, and so on.

Example 133: Arpeggio inversions.

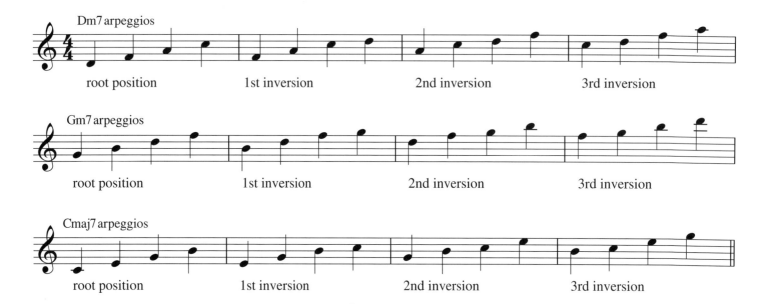

ADVANCED ARPEGGIOS

Since a chord progression is established by the bass player and accompanist, everything a soloist plays is in response to the chords. When an arpeggio is used over a chord, the notes of the arpeggio have a function in relation to the chord. Knowing this, any arpeggio can be played over a chord as long as the notes of the arpeggio are chord tones or acceptable upper partials and alterations. This means an arpeggio does not have to be an active substitute or a passive substitute for the chord. In C Major, for example, the active Dm7 can be played as an arpeggio over the passive Cmaj7 chord. Melodically the arpeggio may be heard as D, F, A, and C, but harmonically the Cmaj7 will be heard as the chord that is part of the chord progression.

DIATONIC EXTENSIONS

An arpeggio that uses the upper partials of the chord is a diatonic extension.

Example 134: An F13 chord functioning as the V chord in B♭ Major.

The arpeggios within the F13 arpeggio are the seven full-diatonic chords of B♭ Major.

The four-part arpeggio for every full-diatonic chord in a key can be derived by using the upper partials of a chord. When any one of the seven arpeggios that are listed in example 134 are played over an F7 chord, the notes sound out either as a chord tone to F7 or an upper partial.

It is very important to know the function and scale choice for a chord to understand when and how an arpeggio is a diatonic extension. The function indicates what the acceptable alterations for the chord are, and the scale generates the natural extensions of the chord. For example, if an E7 chord functioned as a V chord in A Major, an F♯ note would act as a natural extension of the E7. F♯ is diatonic to the key of A Major, and the ninth is a usable upper partial for a V chord in a major key. In contrast, if the E7 chord functioned as the V chord in A Minor, an F♮ note would be a natural extension of E7. F♮ is diatonic to A Harmonic Minor, which is the scale choice for the V chord in a minor key, and is a usable alteration for a V chord in a minor key. So, an extension refers to the addition of any kind of ninth, eleventh, or thirteenth, and natural means it is within the scale that is used. Even though the F♮ is considered a ♭9 over E7, which is an alteration, it is a natural part of the A Harmonic Minor scale. Therefore, when labeling an arpeggio a diatonic extension, it is important to know which notes are in the scale used and which are outside the scale.

Note: Arpeggios can easily be spelled using five or more notes, using the 9th, 11th, or 13th. This is a less common spelling of an arpeggio in jazz, but is certainly present in many artists' solos.

SUPERIMPOSITIONS

An arpeggio that is either partial diatonic or chromatic to the key is considered a superimposition.

There are two basic ways to create an arpeggio that is a superimposition:

1. **Alterations**

   Using the alterations of a chord as a root, 3rd, 5th, or 7th of an arpeggio, a series of superimpositional arpeggios can be created (see page 16 for usable alterations of chords).

Example 135:

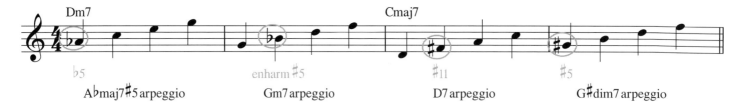

Example 136: Superimpositions created from alterations of a chord.

2. **Minor 3rd Substitution**

   Since a 7th chord can be substituted with another 7th chord that is a minor 3rd apart, an arpeggio of a 7th chord can use the same principle. This also includes tritone substitution, since minor 3rd substitution extended twice is the tritone substitute (see page 26).

Example 137: Minor 3rd substitutes for a B♭7 arpeggio.

The new 7th chord arpeggios can also use any upper partials or alterations in their spellings.

Example 138: Superimpositions for the minor 3rd substitutes of a B♭7 arpeggio.

DEVICES IN ARPEGGIOS

During the bebop era, it was very common to begin every chord change with a chord tone in the solo. If the chord changed to Gmaj7, then the soloist typically played a G (root), B (3rd), D (5th), or F♯ (7th) on the chord change. When the bebop soloist played an arpeggio on a chord change, the first note of the arpeggio would typically be a chord tone as well. However, the arpeggio itself could be a diatonic extension or superimposition over the chord.

Example 139:

It is important to recognize the use of a chord tone on a chord change as a key element of the bebop style, and you should expect to see this in bebop solos. In contrast, the hard bop and hot jazz players preferred beginning a chord change on an upper partial or alteration, and these are equally important elements to look for in solos played during those eras.

MELODIC DEVICES

A jazz improviser will often use specific melodic devices in the development of a solo. These devices create identifiable statements in a solo that are described by their relationship to the other notes of the solo and the chords they are played over. Many of the following devices were adapted to jazz from the classical language. Their addition to the jazz language provided the usage of chromaticism that was generated in the bebop era and continues to be a key element of jazz improvisation. For this reason, many of the following melodic devices are used by jazz players as ways to incorporate chromaticism into their solos, while much of the diatonic playing is better described by the scale choices on the analysis sheets.

ANTICIPATION (ANT):

A chord change is melodically anticipated by playing a chord tone a half or a whole beat early.

Example 140: Anticipations in a III → VI7 → II → V → I progression in F Major.

Example 141: Anticipations in bars 43 through 46 of Miles' solo for "Sippin' at Bells."

NEIGHBOR TONE:

An unstressed non-chord tone that resolves to a chord tone by a major or minor 2nd (a stressed tone is a note occurring on the downbeat and has a duration of a quarter note or longer).

(DNT) Diatonic neighbor tone: The note is part of the scale that is used for the chord.

Example 142: Diatonic neighbor tone.

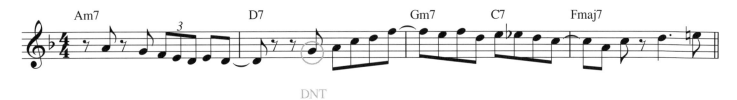

(CNT) Chromatic neighbor tone: The note is outside the scale that is used for the chord.

Example 143: Chromatic neighbor tone.

Example 144: Chromatic neighbor tone in bars 53 through 56 of Miles' solo for "Four."

PASSING TONE

(DPT) Diatonic Passing Tone: Proceeds by scale step connecting chord tones.

Example 145: Diatonic passing tone.

Example 146: Diatonic passing tone in bars 52 through 56 of Miles' solo for "Dig."

(CPT) Chromatic Passing Tone: Proceed by one half step connecting scale tones.

Example 147: Chromatic passing tone.

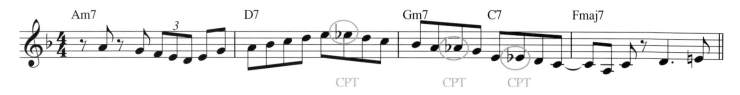

Example 148: Chromatic passing tone in bars 31 through 34 of Miles' solo for "Four."

APPOGGIATURA:

A stressed non-chord tone that resolves to a chord tone by a major or minor 2nd.
   (DAP)–Diatonic appoggiatura
   (CAP)–Chromatic appoggiatura

Example 149: Diatonic appoggiatura.

Example 150: Diatonic appoggiatura in bars 13 through 16 of Miles' solo for "Solar."

Example 151: Chromatic appoggiatura (CAP).

Example 152: Chromatic appoggiatura in bars 21 through 24 of Miles' solo for "My Funny Valentine."

AUXILARY TONE:

A note that connects the same note to itself.
  (DAT)–Diatonic auxilary tone
  (CAT)–Chromatic auxilary tone

Example 153: Diatonic auxilary tone.

Example 154: Chromatic auxilary tone.

Example 155: Diatonic and chromatic auxilary tones in bars 1 through 4 of "Nardis."

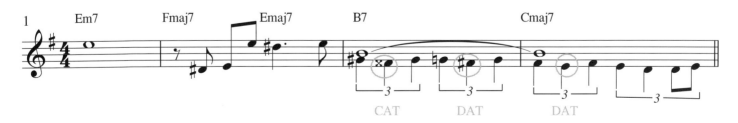

UPPER PARTIAL:

The stressed usage of a 9th, 11th, or 13th that does not resolve to a chord tone. (9), (11), (13)

Example 156: Upper partials.

Example 157: Upper partials in bars 11 through 14 of Miles' solo in "Blue in Green."

ALTERATIONS:

The stressed usage of an alteration that does not resolve to a chord tone. (♭5), (♯5), (♭9), (♯9), (♯11), (♭13)

Example 158: Alterations.

Example 159: Alterations in bars 9 through 12 of Miles' solo for "All Blues."

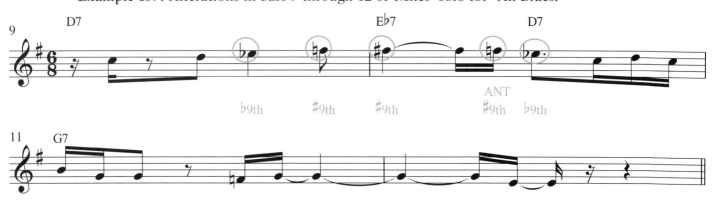

TONE BEHAVIOR

Tone behavior is the natural pressure caused by one note moving to another specific note or notes. On page 24, it was stated that the 7th degree of a key has a natural melodic pull to the octave, and the 4th degree to the 3rd. For a jazz improviser it is important to know the tone behavior of chord alterations. This knowledge gives a soloist precedence for how to incorporate alterations, superimpositions, etc. and use them effectively within a melodic phrase. The following chart lists every chord alteration followed by the chord tones, upper partials, or alterations that best resolve their natural pull or pressure.

Tone behavior of alterations.

♭9	→	root	or	♯9
♯9	→	♭9	or	root
♯11	→	3rd	or	13th
♭5	→	5		
♯5	→	♭5	or	13th
♭13	→	5	or	13

NOTE: This chart provides the typical movement of alterations to other tones in a jazz solo. It is not uncommon to find these alterations move to different tones, often because of a chromatic line.

PART IV
The Solos

SIPPIN' AT BELLS

By Miles Davis

CHARLIE PARKER'S SOLO   MILES' SOLO

© 1948 (Renewed 1975) SCREEN GEMS-EMI MUSIC INC.
All Rights Reserved   International Copyright Secured   Used by Permission

SIPPIN' AT BELLS

KEY: F Major
FORM: Blues

Fmaj7 I	B♭7 IV7 B♭ Mix	Am7 III	Gm7 II	F#m7 II E Major	B7 V
B♭maj7 IV	B♭m7 II A♭ Major	E♭7 V	Am7 III	A♭m7 ♭IIIm7 A♭ Dorian	
Gm7 II	C7 V	Am7 III	D7 VI7 D Mix♭2(♭6)	Gm7 II	G♭7 ♭II7 G♭ Mix#4

THE MUSIC OF MILES DAVIS

"Sippin' at Bells" is a 12-bar head by Miles, and yet is not a traditional 12-bar blues. The post points for a blues (see page 38) are loosely referenced with a I chord in bar 1, a IV chord in bar 5, a III chord as the direct passive substitute for I in bar 7, a II chord as the direct active substitute for V in bar 9, and a III chord in bar 11 again substituting for a I chord. A traditional blues is never established because the I and IV chords are maj7 chords and not 7th chords.

Miles enters a modulation to E Major in bar 4 by moving the Gm7 of bar 3 down chromatically to F#m7. Similarly, the B7 ends the unresolved modulation to E Major, moving chromatically down to B♭maj7, mimicking a ♭II7 → I progression. The B♭m7 acts as an interchange for the B♭maj7, and a modulation to A♭ Major is established in bar 6. Bars 6 through 9 are related to each other by the chromatically descending m7 chords (B♭m7 → Am7 → A♭m7 → Gm7). The progression could easily have created three chromatic descending modulations instead of one.

Example 160:

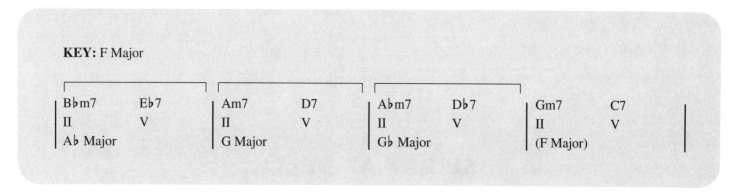

Instead, Miles uses the A♭m7 as ♭IIIm7, which acts as a chromatic chord in F Major. In bar 12, Miles uses the tritone substitution for the V chord (G♭7) in the turnback to the I chord.

Example 161: Head of "Sippin' at Bells."

The melody for "Sippin' at Bells" is typical of a bebop solo. Miles uses several chromatic passing tones in the melody. As is typical in the bebop era, every chord change is melodically accented with a chord tone. In bar 5, Miles uses a Dm7 arpeggio which begins on the 3rd of the chord, B♭maj7. The D♭ arpeggio in bar 10 implies the tritone substitution for C7 (G♭7) using its chord-tone 5th, 7th, and upper-partial 9th.

THE MUSIC OF MILES DAVIS

Example 162: First solo chorus of "Sippin' at Bells."

[Musical notation: Charlie Parker's Solo (bar 13, 24 bars rest) followed by Miles' Solo beginning at Fmaj7, with chord changes Bb7, Am7, Gm7, F#m7, B7, Bbmaj7, Bbm7, Eb7, Am7, Abm7, Gm7, C7, Am7, D7, Gm7, Gb7. Annotations include "4 Notes", "3 Notes", "4 Notes", "3 Notes", "4 Notes", "ANT", "C7 (no root)", "Am7", "ANT".]

    Miles delivered a fairly typical bebop solo, filled with swing eighths and several triplets (a trademark of the bebop style). While Miles used several chromatic passing tones in his melody, there are none in his solo. His first chorus is straightforward, playing right out of the scales we would expect (as he does in the second chorus). In bars 39-41, Miles plays several 3- and 4-note scale runs, almost thematically. The 4-note run in bar 40 is the same run as in bar 39 moved down a half step. In doing this, Miles over-accentuates the modulation to E Major, creating a dissonance in his solo. This is perhaps some indiction that while Miles was becoming a reputed bebop soloist, he was still growing as a musician. In bars 47-48, Miles uses an Am7 arpeggio over the VI7 and II chords (D7 → Gm7). The notes in the arpeggio function over the chords as upper partials.

Example 163: Second solo chorus of "Sippin' at Bells."

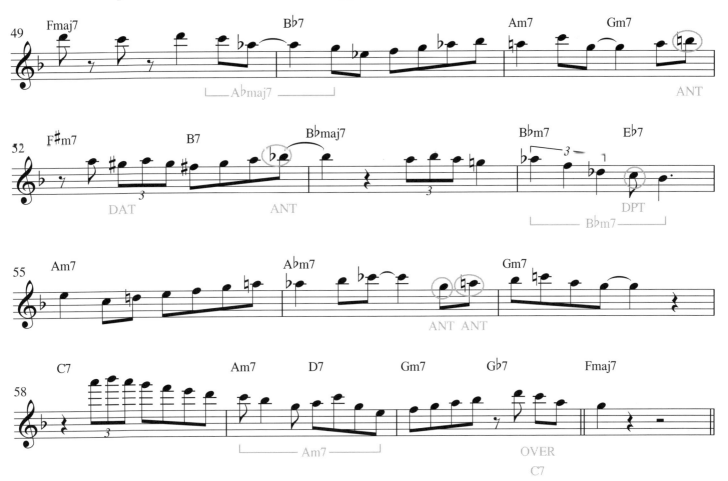

Miles continues the second chorus with another superimposition: an A♭maj7 arpeggio over the B♭7 chord. The notes of the A♭maj7 arpeggio function over the B♭7 chord as: A♭ (7th), C (9th), E♭ (11th), G (13th). The balance of the solo Miles creates lines out of the expected scales. The use of another Am7 arpeggio in bar 59 revisits the usage of the Am7 he used in bars 47-48 of the first chorus. The D, C, and A notes at the end of bar 60 indicate Miles is playing over the V chord (C7) instead of its tritone substitution (G♭7).

THE MUSIC OF MILES DAVIS

MOVE
From the recording *Birth of the Cool* (Miles Davis)

By Denzil De Costa Best

© 1947 (Renewed 1975) BEECHWOOD MUSIC CORP.
All Rights Reserved   International Copyright Secured   Used by Permission

MOVE

KEY: B♭ Major
FORM: AABA

B♭ I	E♭7 IV7 E♭ Mix#4	B♭ I	G7♭9/F VI7 G Mix♭2(♭6)
Cm7 II	F7 V	B♭ I	
B♭ I	E♭7 IV7 E♭ Mix#4	B♭ I	G7♭9/F VI7 G Mix♭2(♭6)
Cm7 II	F7 V	B♭ I	
B♭7 I7 B♭ Mix		E♭maj7 IV	
C7 II7 C Mix		Cm7 II	F7 V
B♭ I	E♭7 IV7 E♭ Mix#4	B♭ I	G7♭9/F VI7 G Mix♭2(♭6)
Cm7 II	F7 V	B♭ I	

MOVE

By Denzil De Costa Best

"Move" reflects Miles' solo style during the cool-jazz era. The song is written in the bebop style and played at a fast tempo. Despite the bebop phrasing in the song, the arrangements and solos take on the laid-back feel of cool jazz. Miles incorporated two important elements into his solo for "Move" that eventually would heavily define his style: use of space and exploiting the tension and color of altered tones and upper partials against a chord.

Example 164: Sections A1 and A2 from Miles' solo on "Move."

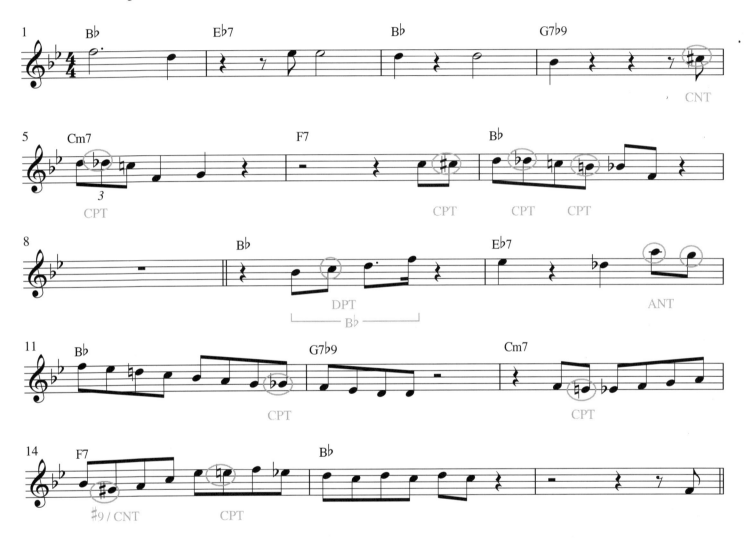

In the first two A sections, Miles uses space (rests) and sustained tones to get a more laid-back feel to the fast tempo. His strong use of chromatic passing tones and chromatic neighbor tones indicate how much the bebop language was still present in the cool-jazz language. The C♯ in bar 4 is a typical example of a bebop phrase where a chromatic neighbor tone becomes a chromatic passing tone (in bar 6).

Example 165: B Section of Miles' solo for "Move."

Miles uses a series of alterations to start the B section, with a repetitive ♯9 and ♭9 against a B♭7 chord. He continues with a ♯11 against the E♭maj7 and ends the phrase with a chromatic appoggiatura, using the 7th against a maj7 chord. All of these tones are usable alterations over the chords, and Miles phrases them for the maximum effect. As his style blossomed in the '50s, his use of alterations and upper partials over chords became a unique aspect of his solos. The chromatic appoggiatura in bar 19 is especially indicative of this, because most players would not use a 7th over a maj7 chord. The effect produced from using alterations and upper partials is that of color and tension against the chord. A 7th over a maj7th (or vice versa) presents more of a clash. Miles wisely uses the 7th (D♭) as an eighth note which quickly resolves to the maj7th (D), providing a unique and unusual effect.

The balance of the B section and solo, Miles plays a bebop style, dominated by continuous swing eighths. The Edim arpeggio in bar 22 is superimposed over C7, acting as the third (E), 5th (G), 7th (B♭), and ♭9 (D♭).

PART IV | THE SOLOS

"DIG" (see page 70 for head analysis)

Miles' solo on "Dig" is a bebop solo which uses more space, like his cool style. His command of the bebop language is more evident here than his days with Charlie Parker. Miles combines long bebop phrases with short thematic phrases, alternating between swing eighths and longer note durations. Miles uses several repeated phrases in his solo, establishing short themes within the solo.

Example 166: Solo motifs in Miles' solo for "Dig."

BARS 1 AND 2

BARS 17 AND 18

BARS 100 AND 101

BARS 122 AND 123

DIG

From the recording *Dig* (Miles Davis)

By Miles Davis

THE MUSIC OF MILES DAVIS

196

Example 167: Solo motifs continued.

BARS 67 AND 68

BARS 82 AND 83

Example 168: Repetitive phrases.

BARS 89 - 92

There are very few arpeggios in the solo. An Em7♭5 arpeggio is superimposed over a B♭7, beginning as a chord-tone 3rd of B♭7 (D), to the root (B♭), 13th (G), and ♯11 (E). Miles often adds passing tones to an arpeggio, as is the case with the Fm arpeggio in bar 21.

Example 169: Bars 21–24 of Miles' solo for "Dig."

There is a good amount of chromaticism in Miles' solo. He also plays between the C Mixolydian ♭2(♭6) scale and a C Mixolydian scale. Some jazz soloists in the early '40s and before used a mixolydian scale over secondary dominant chords instead of the mixolydian ♭2(♭6) scale. Most scales were used according to a strict vertical solution. In other words, a 7th chord would take a mixolydian scale of the same root (C Mixolydian used over C7), a m7 chord would take the dorian scale of the same root (D Dorian over Dm7), etc., regardless of function. As scale usage shifted to the mixolydian ♭2(♭6) over a secondary dominant chord, some soloists found a combination to be also effective. In example 170, Miles is essentially using a C Mixolydian ♭6 over the C7 chord. This allows him to create the Edim7 arpeggio in bar 58, where he avoids the A♭ (♭6 of the scale) altogether. In bar 14, he states the ♭6 (A♭) and the 2nd (D♮), which indicates he is using a C Mix ♭6 for the C7 chord.

Example 170:

BARS 58 AND 59

BARS 14 AND 15

TUNE UP
From the recording *Blue Haze* (Miles Davis)

By Miles Davis

"TUNE UP" (see page 82 for head analysis)

Miles was playing more in the hard-bop style than the bebop style in his solo for "Tune Up." The chromaticism in his solo is much more infrequent than what he used in his bebop solos. He also uses scale substitution and alterations to develop this heavily thematic solo. Miles alludes to the main melody several times in his solo, usually at the end of each chorus. He also uses several repeated phrases throughout the solo, creating short melodic themes as he did in his solo for "Dig."

FOUR

From the recording *Blue Haze* (Miles Davis)

By Miles Davis

"FOUR" (see page 85 for head analysis)

Much like Miles' solo on "Tune Up," "Four" uses melody quotes, thematic repetition, and scale substitution.

SOLAR

From the recording *Walkin'* (Miles Davis)

By Miles Davis

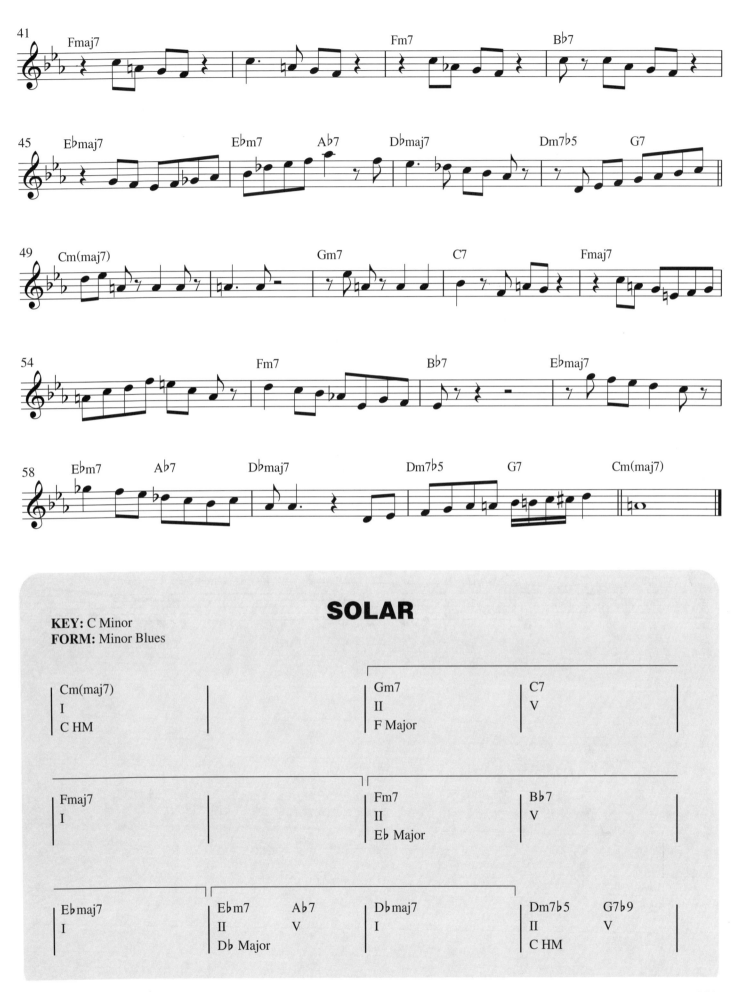

"SOLAR"

"Solar" is an unlikely minor blues. The bulk of the 12 bars is spent in modulation away from the main key of C Minor, and yet the song has a slow, blues feel. Miles begins the song with the I chord from the C Harmonic Minor scale, Cm(maj7). He modulates to F Major using the V chord of C Natural Minor (Gm7), with the Gm7 acting as the II chord in F Major. He proceeds with two more modulations that are entered and exited with tonic interchanges (Fmaj7 becomes Fm7, and E♭maj7 becomes E♭m7). The root of the I chord of the final modulation to Dmaj7 rises chromatically to the root of Dm7♭5 (the II chord of the main key [C Minor]).

Example 171: "Solar" (head only).

The main motif for "Solar" is established in bars 1-4. This motif is entirely in C Tonic Minor, although the chord modulates to F Major in bars 3 and 4. Bars 5-8 are a variation on the first motif. Bar 5 continues in C Tonic Minor, with the addition of a ♯9th in the melody. Bars 6-8 shift to using C Natural Minor in the melody, or the relative major (E♭ Major), since the chords modulate to E♭ Major. Bars 9-11 provide the second motif which utilizes a descending chromatic line in the first notes of each bar (G → G♭ → F). The turnback in bar 12 initially implies C Major with an E♮ in the scale run, shifting to C Natural Minor on beats 3 and 4. Certainly the ambiguity of the key is reinforced when the song repeats with the I chord in C Harmonic Minor instead of C Natural Minor.

"SOLAR": THE SOLO

Example 172: Solo motifs.

Example 173: Melody quotes in Miles' solo for "Solar."

BARS 13 AND 14

BARS 33 - 36

BARS 57 - 60

Example 174: Arpeggios in Miles' solo for "Solar."

BARS 17 AND 18

BARS 46 AND 47

BARS 53 AND 54

"VIERD BLUES"

"Vierd Blues" is a basic blues in B♭ major, with the addition of a II chord in Bar 9 (substituting for the V), and a II → V turnback in bar 12. The melody has one main motif, which oddly enough uses a maj7 in the melody against the 7th chord.

Example 175: "Vierd Blues" (head only).

VIERD BLUES

From the recording *Collector's Items* (Miles Davis)

By Miles Davis

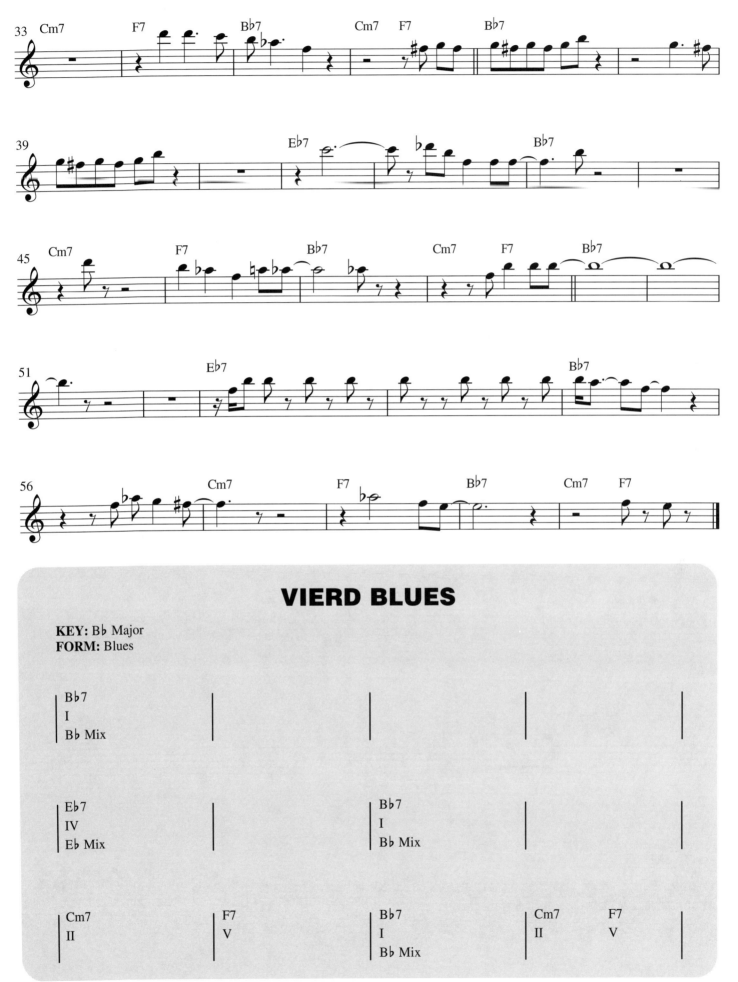

VIERD BLUES

KEY: B♭ Major
FORM: Blues

B♭7 I B♭ Mix				
E♭7 IV E♭ Mix		B♭7 I B♭ Mix		
Cm7 II	F7 V	B♭7 I B♭ Mix	Cm7 II	F7 V

"VIERD BLUES:" THE SOLO

Miles' entire solo for "Vierd Blues" is developed using a mixture of a B♭ Blues and B♭ Pentatonic scale: B♭ C D♭ D E♭ F G A♭.

Example 176: Miles' first and second solo chorus for "Vierd Blues."

There are three repetitive phrases Miles uses in his solo.

Example 177:

BARS 21 AND 22

BARS 36 - 39

BARS 53 - 55

MY FUNNY VALENTINE
from BABES IN ARMS
From the recording *Cookin'* (Miles Davis)

Words by Lorenz Hart
Music by Richard Rodgers

MY FUNNY VALENTINE

KEY: C Minor
FORM: AABA

Cm7	Dm7b5	G7	Cm7	F7
I	II	V	I	IV7
C NM	C HM		C NM	F Mix

Abmaj7		Gm7	Fm6	Dm7b5	G7
VI		Vm7	IVm6	II	V
C NM		C NM	F Dorian	C HM	

Cm7	Dm7b5	G7	Cm7	F7
I	II	V	I	IV7
C NM	C HM		C NM	F Mix

Abmaj7	Am7b5	D7	Gm7	C7	Fm7	Bb7
VI	II	V	II	V	IV / II	V
C NM	G HM		F Major		Eb Major	

Ebmaj7	Fm7	Gm7	Fm7	Ebmaj7	Fm7	Gm7	Fm7
I	II	III	II	I	II	III	II

Ebmaj7	Dm7b5	G7	Cm7	Cb7	Bbm7	Eb7	Abmaj7	Dm7b5	G7
I	II	V	I		II	V	I / VI	II	V
	C HM		C NM		Ab Major			C HM	

Cm7	Dm7b5	G7	Cm7	F7
I	II	V	I	IV7
C NM	C HM		C NM	F Mix

Abmaj7	Dm7b5	G7	Cm7	Cb7	Bbm7	Eb7
VI	II	V	I		II	V
C NM	C HM		C NM		Ab Major	

Abmaj7	Gm7	Gb7	Fm7	Bb7	Ebmaj7	Fm7	Gm7	Dm7b5	G7
I	III		II	V	I	II	III	II	V
	Eb Major							C HM	

Cm7	Dm7b5	

THE MUSIC OF MILES DAVIS

"MY FUNNY VALENTINE" (see page 42 for analysis of original version)

Miles made numerous chord changes and freely improvised the melody to "My Funny Valentine." Miles regularly would improvise the melodies to standards, such that the original melody was barely present but a beautiful, striking solo stood in its place. Eventually, many of Miles' melodies for his own songs were more of an improvisation than a predetermined melody.

Example 178: Original A section of "My Funny Valentine."

Example 179: Miles' A section of "My Funny Valentine."

The first changes Miles made to the chord progression of "My Funny Valentine" (refer to pages 45-47 for complete analysis) are the II → V in bar 2 and the IV7 in bar 4. These chords can still carry the chromatic line that the original four chords created (C → B → B♭ → A) and add even more momentum to the progression itself.

The Gm7 in bar 6 acts as the Vm7, the natural V chord of the C Natural Minor scale. The Dm7♭5 substitutes for the Fm chord in bar 8 to create a II → V progression. The melody in A1 is the closest Miles gets to stating the original melody. Bars 1-4 state the notes of the original theme, although they are rhythmically displaced. The boxes over notes in bars 4-8 indicate when Miles has played, in some way, part of the original melody. Miles makes a striking use of 4th intervals in his improvisation on this melody, which we see for the first time in bars 6-8 (B♭ up to E♭, down to B♭, down to F).

Example 180: Miles' section **A2** of "My Funny Valentine."

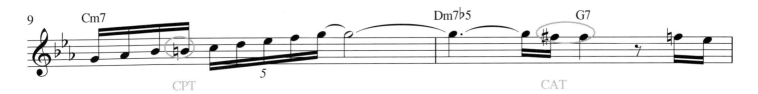

In the second A section, Miles adds two modulations in bar 14, and uses an Fm7 in bar 15 instead of the original A♭m. The A♭m is the chord-tone 3rd (A♭), 5th (C), and 7th (E♭) of Fm7. However, using the Fm7 creates a stronger root movement into the relative major, E♭ Major (F → B♭ → E♭).

The boxes again indicate the original melody, which as you can see, Miles has largely abandoned. In bars 1-3, he creates one of his trademark lines that creates dissonance and resolves to a consonant note. In this case, Miles sustains a G in bar 9, which acts as the 5th of C7 and then the 11th of Dm7♭5. He moves down a half step to play F♯ in bar 10. The F♯ is not only dissonant against the G7 (pitting a maj7 against a 7th), but melodically leaves C Minor as well. The F♯ looks as if it is resolved at the F♮, functioning as a chromatic passing tone. However, audibly the F♯ is resolved when the G is played in bar 11, so the F♯ functions as a chromatic auxiliary tone (CAT) between the G♮ of bar 9 and the G♮ in bar 11.

Example 181: "Jazz changes" to the B section of "My Funny Valentine."

Example 182: Miles' B section of "My Funny Valentine."

Miles used what was considered the "jazz changes" to "My Funny Valentine" for the B section. The addition of Dm7♭5 in bar 21 adds some momentum to the V chord (G7). The C♭7 in bar 22 is a chromatic passing chord used by Red Garland. It connects the root of Cm7 to the root of B♭m7 (C → C♭ → B♭). This is a chord Red Garland undoubtedly added as the song was being played, and clearly Miles does not respond to the chord in his melody. Passing chords and chord substitutions by the accompanist are important to understand solo analysis, because these chords are usually not the chords the soloist is playing over. This is especially critical with a player like Miles, who used more individual notes to color a chord and construct his solo.

Miles makes no reference to the original melody in the B section. Instead, his solo uses short motifs and sustained notes to create a remarkably melodic solo in this section.

PART IV | THE SOLOS

Example 183: "Jazz changes" for section A3 of "My Funny Valentine."

Example 184: Miles' section A3 of "My Funny Valentine."

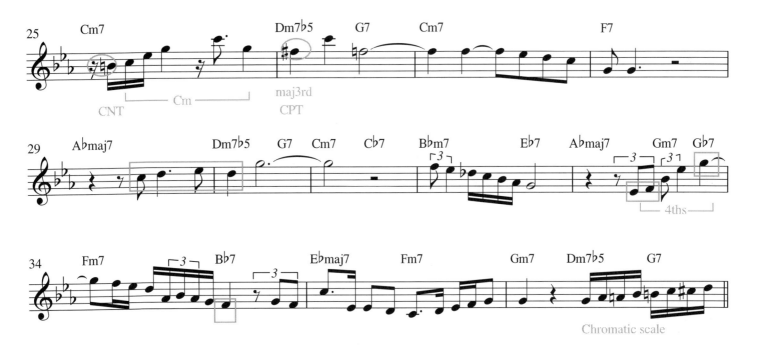

Miles uses a combination of his A1 section, the A3 of the common jazz changes, and the B section to create the A3 chord changes for his version of "My Funny Valentine."

Bars 1–4: the chords from Miles' section A1.
Bars 5–8: from the "jazz changes" for "My Funny Valentine."
Bars 9–12: the "jazz changes" are embellished with elements of Miles' B section in the modulation to E♭ major.

Miles' solo barely states the original melody. In bar 26, Miles again is playing with consonance and dissonance, using a maj3rd (F♯) over the m3rd of Dm7♭5 (F). The F♯ acts as a chromatic passing tone between the G♮ in bar 25 and the F♮ in bar 26. He again uses intervals of a 4th in his solo, giving a feeling of suspension in the melody.

223

THE MUSIC OF MILES DAVIS

TUNE UP
From the recording *Cookin'* (Miles Davis)

By Miles Davis

Copyright © 1963 Prestige Music
Copyright Renewed
International Copyright Secured   All Rights Reserved

"TUNE UP" (see page 82 for head analysis)

This version of "Tune Up' is from Miles' album *Cookin'*. It is significantly different from his previous version on *Blue Haze*. the melody references are gone and the repetitive solo motifs are fewer. In this solo, Miles makes extreme use of chromaticism, especially chromatic passing tones and chromatic auxilary tones. His solo is comprised of long phrases made of scales and few arpeggios. He also uses several scale substitutions in this solo, in no doubt partly influenced by Coltrane, who was part of his working band by now.

SID'S AHEAD

From the recording *Milestones* (Miles Davis)

By Miles Davis

PART IV | THE SOLOS

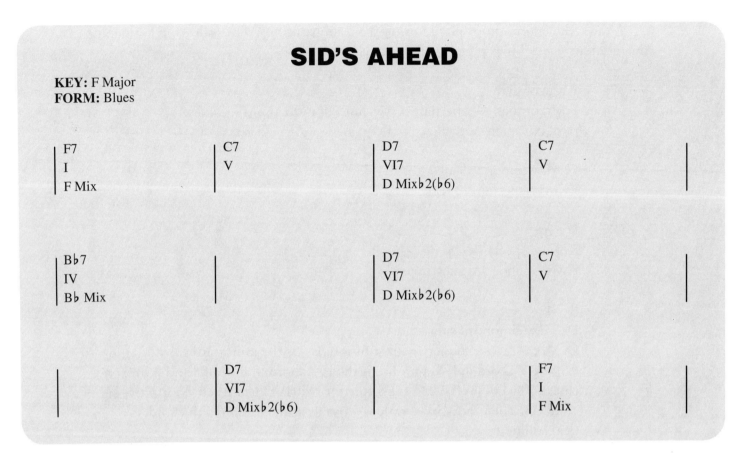

"SID'S AHEAD"

"Sid's Ahead" is another basic blues with added chords. The D7 chord acts as the minor 3rd substitution for the I chord (F7) in bars 7 and 10. There is only one motif that is repeated and varied to construct the melodic theme.

Example 185: "Sid's Ahead" (head only).

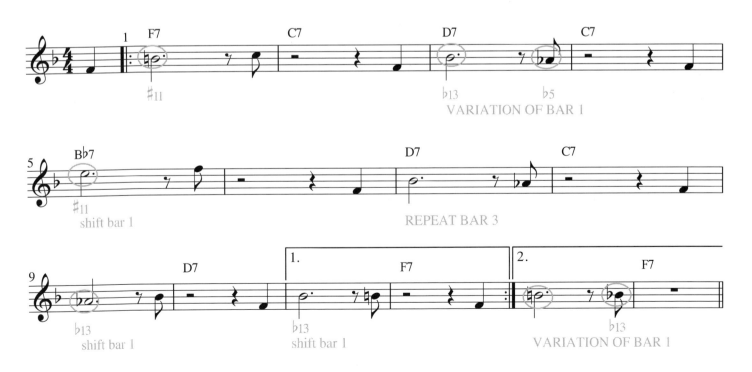

Almost the entire solo is played using scale substitutions. The following list details the different scales Miles preferred for each chord:

- F7: F Mixolydian
  F Mixolydian ♯4–alternate scale choice for 7th chord
  B♭ Mixolydian–specialized scale

- C7: E♭ Mix–minor 3rd substitute
  A♭ Mix–specialized scale

- D7: D Mix
  B♭ Mix–specialized scale
  F Mix–minor 3rd substitute

- B♭7: B♭ Mix
  D♭ Mix–minor 3rd substitute
  E♭ Mix ♯4–active for active substitution. E♭7 is the minor 3rd substitute for C7, the V chord in F Major. B♭7 is the IV7 chord in F Major and is an active chord. The E♭7 (♭VII7) can substitute for B♭7 (IV7) using active for active substitution. Then the Mix ♯4 scale is a usable scale over any 7th chord as a vertical solution.

The Mixolydian and Mixolydian ♯4 scales with the same root as the chord (F Mix or F Mix ♯4 over F7, for example) are both usable as scales that directly fit a 7th chord (see page 162). The minor 3rd substitution principle that works for chords (see page 25) is applicable to scales as well, especially 7th chords. The minor 3rd substitutes of C7, for example, are E♭7, G♭7, and A7. Typical scale solutions for each chord are: C Mix, E♭ Mix, G♭ Mix, and A Mix. Knowing the chords are interchangeable, then the scales are as well. This produces an interesting effect because the soloist usually substitutes the scale while the accompanist still plays the original chord. In the case of "Sid's Ahead," one of the chords played is C7 while Miles uses the minor 3rd scale substitute E♭ Mix over the top.

The third type of scale Miles substituted is indicated as a "specialized scale". This is because there is not a specific substitution principle that is used in the creation of this substitution scale. The scale is derived from usable upper partials and alterations of a 7th chord. In the case of the C7 chord, the ♭5, ♯5, ♭9, and ♯9 are employed. The scale uses the root, ♭9, ♯9, 4, ♭5, ♯5, and 7th of a 7th chord. For a C7 chord this would be: C D♭ E♭ F G♭ A♭ B♭. This scale could easily be perceived as D♭ Major, C Locrian, E♭ Dorian, etc., but since it is used to specifically embellish a 7th chord, it is named from a mixolydian scale: A♭ Mixolydian. Miles uses the same type of substitutions over the D7 chord (the mixolydian scale whose root is an augmented 5th away: B♭ Mixolydian). The scale substitution allows many blue notes to enter into the solo, and is a scale substitution seen in the solos of Miles' band members, like Red Garland, who always had a strong blues feel in his playing.

MILES

From the recording *Milestones* (Miles Davis)

By Miles Davis

"MILES" (see page 106 for head analysis)

"Miles" is Miles' first completely modal song. His solo is developed strictly out of two modes: G Dorian and A Dorian. Miles follows Cannonball Adderly in order of soloists on the recording, and the first phrase of Miles' solo mirrors Cannonball Adderly's last phrase. Playing strictly in one mode for an extended period of time allows for an exceptionally lyrical solo from Miles, as was Cannonball Adderly's solo. In the first solo chorus, Miles plays phrases that constantly resolve to a sustained G note in G Dorian or a sustained A or D (11th) note in A Dorian.

Example 186: Section A1 in G Dorian and bars 17-24 of the B section in A Dorian.

BARS 1-8

QUOTE FROM Cannonball Adderly's solo

BARS 17-24

In the second solo chorus, Miles continues with some of the same ideas as in the first chorus. Notes are resolved and sustained (G and D over Gm7, A and D again over Am7). Chromaticism also enters into the solo, with the addition of the chromatic auxilary tone G♯ in bars 46-50, used to emphasize the A note. Throughout the solo, Miles' use of triplets and sustained notes gives a rhythmic theme to the solo and a slow, loping feel to an up-tempo song.

Example 187: Bars 46-50 of Miles' solo for "Miles."

SO WHAT
From the recording *Kind of Blue* (Miles Davis)

By Miles Davis

THE MUSIC OF MILES DAVIS

"SO WHAT" (see page 112 for head analysis)

"So What" follows in the idea of "Miles" as a song composed with two different dorian scales: D Dorian and E♭ Dorian. In the first 16 bars of Miles' solo, he makes a strong point to play the chord tones of Dm7.

Example 188: Bars 1 through 16 of "So What."

Also established in bars 1 through 16 is Miles' way of accenting phrases in this solo with a note played twice at the end of a phrase in a specific rhythmic pattern. This way of ending each phrase is present throughout Miles' solo, and in a way ties the entire solo together as the main motif.

"BLUE IN GREEN"

"Blue in Green" is, for the most part, a 10-bar theme. The melody in the first 10 bars is most likely an improvisation by Miles, which continues into the next chorus. Most versions of this head show the basic melody as a simplified version of Miles' solo.

Example 189: Head to "Blue in Green."

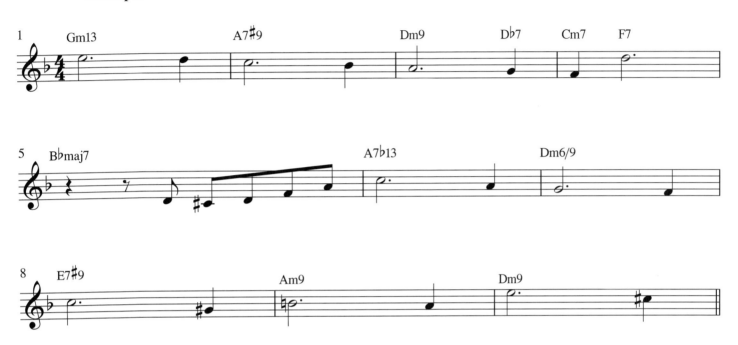

BLUE IN GREEN
From the recording *Kind of Blue* (Miles Davis)

By Miles Davis

BLUE IN GREEN

KEY: D Minor
FORM: 10 Bars

Gm7	A7#9	Dm7		Cm7	F7
IV	V	I / III	bIII7	II	V
D HM		D NM	Db Mix#4	Bb Major	

Bbmaj7	A7	Dm6/9	E7b9
I / VI	V	Im6	V
D NM	D HM	D Dorian	A HM

Am7	Dm7
I	IV / I
A NM	D NM

The chords for the song were evidently a sketch of chords that Miles gave to Bill Evans to further organize. The authorship of the song has long been disputed between that of Miles (who is credited with the song) or Bill Evans. The chords for "Blue in Green" more strongly reflect the style of Bill Evans. Evans' songs were tightly constructed using full diatonic pivot chords to enter and exit modulations (as is true with "Blue in Green"). Also, a trademark of Evans was the progression of m7th chords in fourths, which mimics a repetitive I → IV/I → IV/I → etc. in minor keys. This is clear in bars 9 and 10 and the return to bar 1. This is evident in some of Evans' songs, specifically "Time Remembered."

Example 190:

Am7	Dm7	Gm7	Cm7
I	IV / I	IV / I	IV / I

"Blue in Green" is played at a very slow tempo, with Jimmy Cobb maintaining a steady tempo on the drums throughout. The chord progression, however, is played double and triple time in the middle of the song. As Miles' first solo ends, Evans and Coltrane take a solo with the chords played double time.

Example 191: The chords of "Blue in Green" played double time.

At the end of Coltrane's solo, Evans plays another solo with the chords played triple time. This is continued 2 bars into Miles' return, and then returns to the original chord placement in 10 bars.

Example 192: The chords of "Blue in Green" played triple time.

Miles' solo is very lyrical and melodic, which he was always known for on ballads. While Miles doesn't establish any repetitive motifs within his solo, the impression of one long theme is felt in this well-developed solo. Miles does use several scale substitutions in "Blue in Green." Unlike "Tune Up" (*Cookin'*) and "Sid's Ahead," where Miles used scale substitution to get a more "outside" feel to his solo, his scale substitution in "Blue in Green" is allowing for more color tones over the chords without losing the integrity of the chords.

Example 193: Bars 57-70 of Miles' solo for "Blue in Green."

ALL BLUES

From the recordings *Kind of Blue* and
The Complete Concert 1964 (My Funny Valentine + Four & More) (Miles Davis)

By Miles Davis

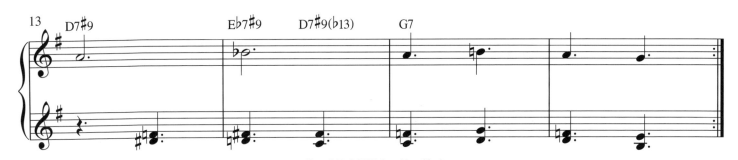

Copyright © 1959 Jazz Horn Music
Copyright Renewed
All Rights Administered by Sony/ATV Music Publishing, 8 Music Square West, Nashville, TN 37203
International Copyright Secured   All Rights Reserved

ALL BLUES
From the recording *Kind of Blue* (Miles Davis)

By Miles Davis

ALL BLUES

KEY: G Major
FORM: Blues

G7				
I				
G Mix				

C7		G7		
IV		I		
C Mix		G Mix		

D7	E♭7　　D7	G7		
V	♭VI7　　V	I		
	E♭ Mix♯4	G Mix		

"ALL BLUES"

"All Blues" is a basic blues with the addition of a ♭VI7 chord in bar 10. The melody is made up of two motifs.

Example 194: "All Blues" (Head).

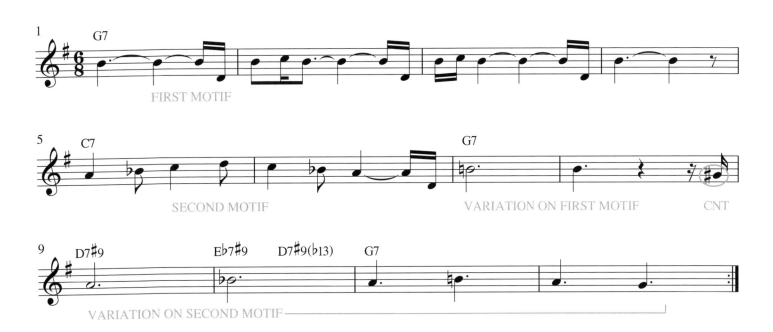

"ALL BLUES": THE SOLO

SO WHAT
From the recording *At Carnegie Hall* (Miles Davis)

By Miles Davis

THE MUSIC OF MILES DAVIS

"SO WHAT" (see page 112 for head analysis)

This solo of "So What" is very different from Miles' original solo on *Kind of Blue*. The feel is closer to the aggressive hard-bop solos Miles played on *Milestones* and less lyrical than the original version. His use of melody quotes and solo motifs are sparser than usual for this time period, favoring long solo lines and a good amount of chromaticism. This is from a live performance at Carnegie Hall, which may have inspired Miles to play more aggressively.

Example 195: Solo motifs.

Example 196: Repetitive phrases in Miles' solo for "So What."

Example 197: Chromaticism in Miles' solo for "So What."

MY FUNNY VALENTINE
from BABES IN ARMS
From the recording
The Complete Concert 1964 (My Funny Valentine + Four & More) (Miles Davis)

Words by Lorenz Hart
Music by Richard Rodgers

MY FUNNY VALENTINE

KEY: C Minor
FORM: AABA

Cm	Cm(maj7)	Cm7	Cm6
I	Im(maj7)	I	Im6
C NM	C HM	C NM	C Dorian

Abmaj7	Fm7	Dm7b5 G7	
VI	IV	II V	
C NM	C NM	C HM	

Cm	Cm(maj7)	Cm7	Cm6
I	IM(maj7)	I	Im6
C NM	C HM	C NM	C Dorian

Abmaj7	Am7 Gm7	Fm7b5	Bb7
VI	III II / III	IIm7b5	V
C NM	F Major	F Locrian	Eb Major

Ebmaj9 Dbmaj9	Ebmaj9 Dbmaj9	Ebmaj9 Dbmaj9	Ebmaj9 Dbmaj9
I bVIImaj7	I bVIImaj7	I bVIImaj7	I bVIImaj7
Db Lydian	Db Lydian	Db Lydian	Db Lydian

Ebmaj7 Dm7b5 Db7	Cm7 F7	Bbm7 A7 Abmaj7	Dm7b5 G7
I II bII7	I IV7	II V I / VI	II V
C HM Db Mix#4	C NM F Mix	Ab Major A Mix#4	C HM

Cm	Cm(maj7)	Cm7	Cm6
I	Im(maj7)	I	Im6
C NM	C HM	C NM	C Dorian

Abmaj7 Dm7b5 G7	Cm7 F7	Bbm7 Eb7	Abmaj7
VI II V	I IV7	II V	I / IV
C NM C HM	C NM F Mix	Ab Major	

	Fm7	Bb7	Eb	
	II	V	I	II V
	Eb Major			C HM

"MY FUNNY VALENTINE" (see page 42 for analysis of original head)

The chords for this version of "My Funny Valentine" are almost entirely those of the common jazz changes (see page 49). The most unique chord additions are in the B section. The original changes were made up of a repetitive II → V → I in the B section (see page 41). In this version, the V chord of the B section (B♭7 in the key of E♭ Major) is replaced with its minor 3rd substitute, D♭7. However, as was very popular during this era, ♭VII7 and ♭II7 chords were frequently played as maj7 chords. So, the progression for Miles' B section is made up of a ♭VIImaj7 → I progression, adding more color to the original progression.

The song begins without any tempo (rubato), and Miles sparsely alludes to the original melody.

The band begins playing in tempo (a tempo) in bar 31, just before the first chorus. At this time, the duration of each chord doubles, such that a chord that lasted only 1 bar now lasts 2. For simplicity, the analysis sheet shows the chords in their original 36-bar structure, as opposed to Miles' version, which becomes a 72-bar structure. As this is a version from a live performance, Miles' solo alternates between his highly developed thematic approach, and more aggressive playing in response to the energy of the band and the audience (much as we had seen in his solo for "So What" at Carnegie Hall). Miles' solo is more descript of his work with alterations in direct response to the chords, and is not derivative of scale substitution as he often used.

Example 198: Solo motifs.

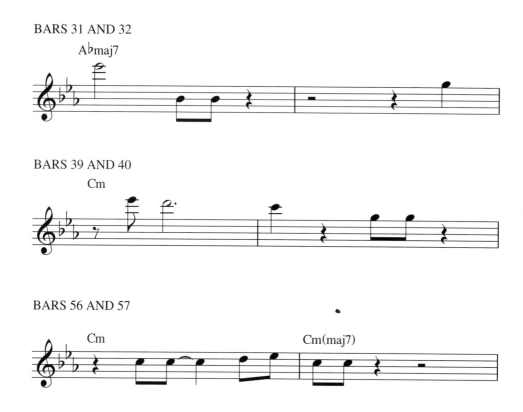

BARS 43 AND 44: A motif/similar phrase from Miles' solo on "So What" at Carnegie Hall.

BARS 91 AND 92

BARS 106 AND 107

Example 199: Miles' use of **alterations** over the chords of "My Funny Valentine."

BARS 41 AND 42

BARS 47 AND 48

BARS 57 AND 58

BARS 66 AND 67

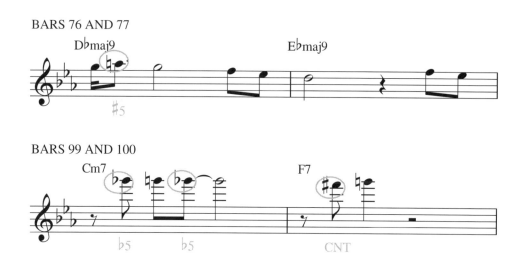

Example 200: Miles' use of **chromaticism** in his solo for "My Funny Valentine."

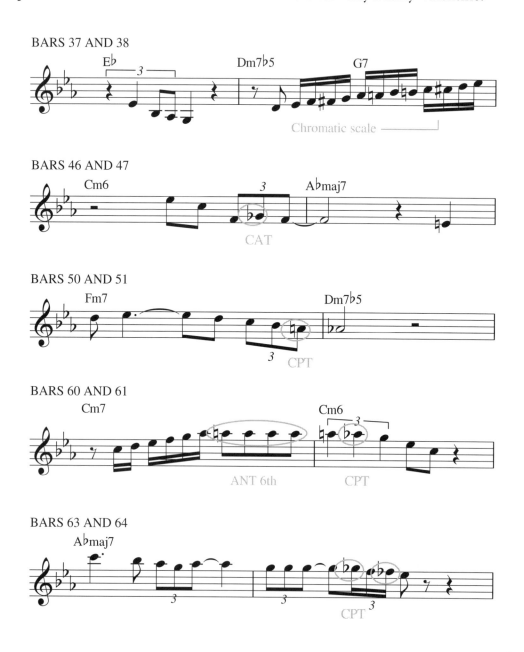

Example 201: Miles' **intervallic use of fourths** in his solo for "My Funny Valentine" (a divice he used in the *Cookin'* version as well).

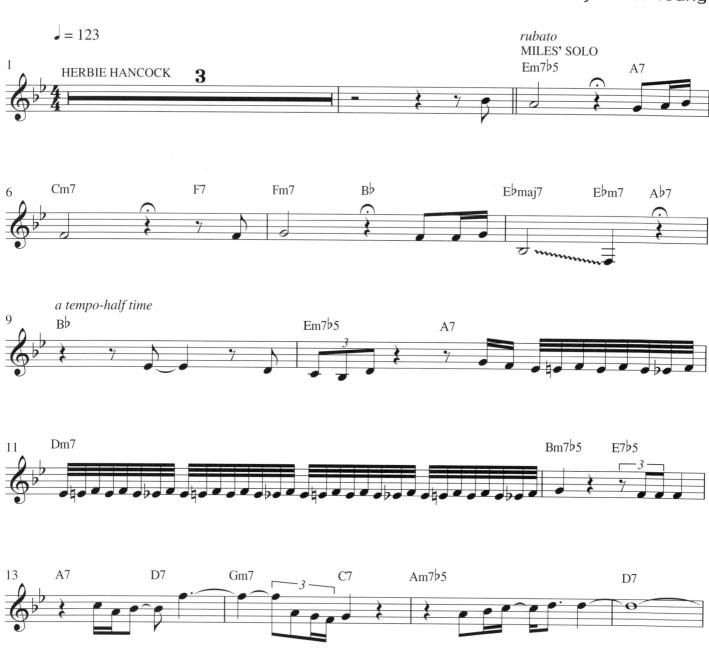

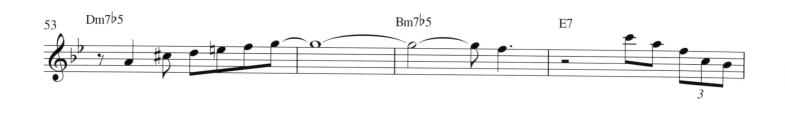

PART IV | THE SOLOS

STELLA BY STARLIGHT

KEY: B♭ Major
FORM: AB

Em7♭5	A7	Cm7	F7
II	V	II	V
D HM			

Fm7	B♭7	E♭maj7	E♭m7	A♭7
II	V	I	II	V / ♭VII7
E♭ Major			D♭ Major	

B♭	Em7♭5	A7	Dm7	Bm7♭5	E7(♭5)
I	II	V	I	II	V
	D HM		D NM	A HM	

A7	D7	Gm7	C7	Am7♭5	D7
III7	VI7	II	V	II	V
A Mix	D Mix♭2(♭6)	F Major		G HM	

G+7		Cm7	
VI7		II	
G Mix♭2(♭6)			

A♭7		B♭maj7	F7
♭VII7		I	V
A♭ Mix#4			

Em7♭5	A7	Dm7♭5	G7
II	V	II	V
D HM		C HM	

Cm7♭5	F7	B♭maj7	F7
IIm7♭5	V	I	V
B♭ HM			

"STELLA BY STARLIGHT"

"Stella by Starlight" was another favorite ballad of Miles. This version is from the 1964 concert as "My Funny Valentine" and is structured in much the same way. The melody begins rubato, switches to half-time, and before the first chorus it reaches regular tempo. There are spots in "Stella by Starlight" that the band cuts and doubles the time, so the analysis sheet reflects the standard 32-bar version of the song without regard for the altered tempos.

"Stella by Starlight" was a well-covered jazz standard, and Miles was one of many jazz artists to have recorded the song. On the following page is the common set of jazz chords for "Stella by Starlight" with the original melody.

Miles' version makes a few modifications to these chord changes:

1. In **bar 8** Miles uses an interchange (E♭m7 for E♭maj7) to establish a brief modulation to D♭ Major using the original A♭7 chord.

2. In **bars 12-14** Miles creates a root movement in fourths (B → E → A → G → C) from the chords, and establishes a modulation to F Major in bars 13 and 14.

3. F7 in **bars 24 and 32** is the V chord of the main key (B♭ Major), and its root moves chromatically down to the E♮ root of Em7♭5 to enter the modulations to D Minor.

STELLA BY STARLIGHT
from the Paramount Picture THE UNINVITED
Jazz Changes

Words by Ned Washington
Music by Victor Young

PART IV | THE SOLOS

Miles makes several references to the original melody in his version, while still freely improvising over the chords in other parts.

Example 202: Bars 1-20 of Miles' solo for "Stella by Starlight."

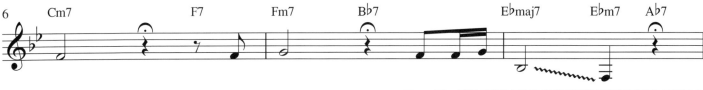

285

THE MUSIC OF MILES DAVIS

Miles uses scale substitution and alterations throughout his solo for "Stella by Starlight." Much of this is used to create dissonance instead of color, such that he alternates between beautiful melodic statements and dissonant contrasts. Many of the alterations are also due to Miles playing flat, so that the note he states is microtonal (in between a half step or in between E and F, for example).

Example 203: Miles' use of **chromaticism** in his solo for "Stella by Starlight."

BARS 25 AND 26

BARS 69 AND 70

PART IV | THE SOLOS

Example 204: Miles' use of **scale substitution** in his solo for "Stella by Starlight."

IRIS
From the recording *E.S.P.* (Miles Davis)

By Wayne Shorter

IRIS

KEY: E♭ Major
FORM: 16 Bars

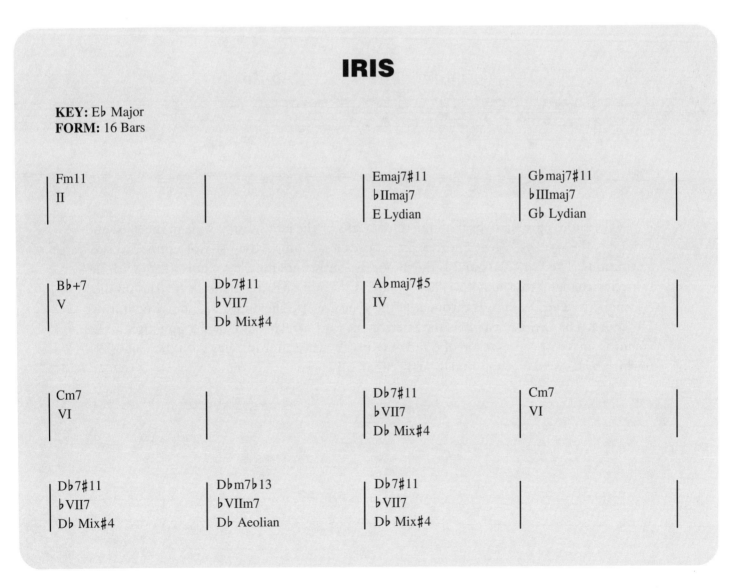

"IRIS"

Example 205: "Iris" (head only).

The chords for "Iris" bear all the trademarks of the jazz writing style in the '60s, and notably the style of Wayne Shorter. The chords are comprised mostly of minor 3rd substitutions. The Emaj7 in bar 2 is the minor 3rd substitute for the V chord (Bb7) with the species changed to a maj7th. The Gbmaj7 is the minor 3rd substitute for the implied Ebmaj7 (I). The Db7 chords throughout the song are also the minor 3rd substitute for the V chord. The Dbm7 in bar 14 is the interchange for Db7. The bulk of the song uses active chords (or substitutions thereof), and only uses passive chords twice with the Cm7 (VI), which has a weaker resolutional quality than a I chord.

"Iris" is a slow ballad, and the melody is developed as one theme that stretches over all 16 bars. All of the chords are altered such that the melody functions more directly over the chords as either a chord tone, upper partial, or alteration. While the melody and chords are certainly unusual, the listener is never left with the impression of dissonance. The song and solos come across as a colorful ballad, showing the strength of both the writing ability and the players on the recording. Miles incorporates four main ideas into his solo in "Iris."

1. As "Iris" is a ballad, Miles spends much of his time playing within the scales and utilizing chord tones and upper partials for color to create beautiful phrases.

2. He also uses a good deal of space to separate ideas and let the phrases breathe.

Example 206: Miles' **first solo chorus** for "Iris."

THE MUSIC OF MILES DAVIS

3. Miles uses alterations and alternate scales to almost intentionally create dissonance or tension to contrast his other, more diatonic lines.

4. Miles adds a lot of chromaticism to this solo. But, he places the chromatic notes in quick runs that connect diatonic notes. These chromatic passages provide movement in the phrases with sustained notes and loping rhythms.

Example 207: Miles' **solo chorus**' 3-5 for "Iris."

CIRCLE

From the recording *Miles Smiles* (Miles Davis)

By Miles Davis

CIRCLE

KEY: D Minor

Dm7		Dm6	Bbmaj7b5
I		Im6	VI / I
D NM		D Dorian	D NM

Ebmaj7b5	D13	Bm9	Cmaj7
IV	V	III	IV
Eb Lydian	G Major		

root cycle asc. minor 2nd

		Gmaj7	Abmaj7
		I /	
			Ab Major

A7sus4	Fmaj7b5	A7sus4	
/ V	III	V	
D HM	D NM	D HM	

Dmaj7		Bbmaj7b5	
Imaj7		VI	
D Major		D NM	

Em7b5	A7	Dm7	
II	V	I	
D HM		D NM	

Dm6	Bbmaj7b5	Ebmaj7b5	D13
Im6	VI / I	IV	V
D Dorian	D NM	Eb Lydian	G Major

| Bm9 | Cmaj7 | | |
| III | IV | | |

```
                    root cycle asc. minor 2nd
| Gmaj7        | A♭maj7      | A7sus4      | Fmaj7♭5     |
| I /          |             | / V         | III         |
| G Major      | A♭ Major    | D HM        | D NM        |

| A7sus4       |             | Dmaj7       |             |
| V            |             | Imaj7       |             |
| D HM         |             | D Major     |             |

| Gm7          |             | F7sus4      | F7♭9        |
| IV           |             | V           |             |
| D NM         |             | B♭ Major    |             |

| B♭maj7♭5     |             | E♭maj7♭5    | A7          |
| I            |             | IV          | V           |
|              |             |             | D HM        |

| Dm7          |             | Dm6         | B♭maj7♭5    |
| I            |             | Im6         | VI / I      |
| D NM         |             | D Dorian    | D NM        |

| Emaj7♭5      | D13         | Bm9         | Cmaj7       |
| IV           | V           | III         | IV          |
| E♭ Lydian    | G Major     |             |             |

                              root cycle asc. minor 2nd
|              |             | Gmaj7       | A♭maj7      |
|              |             | I /         |             |
|              |             |             | A♭ Major    |

| A7sus4       | Fmaj7♭5     | A7sus4      |             |
| / V          | III         | V           |             |
| D HM         | D NM        | D HM        |             |
```

THE MUSIC OF MILES DAVIS

"CIRCLE"

"Circle" is a ballad from Miles, written with an advanced chord progression in the style of jazz in the 1960s. There is no song form for "Circle," as the song is constructed from one long chord progression. The first 18 bars have the only recurring chord progression which is followed each time by a different progression of unequal bar lengths.

Example 208: Bars 1-18 of "Circle."

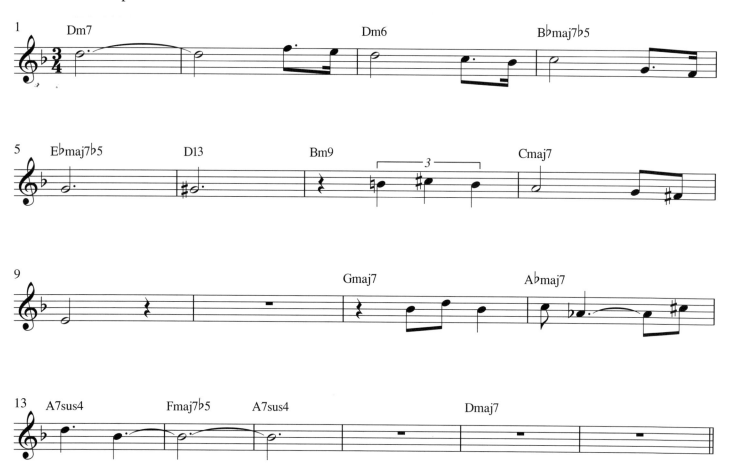

Methods of modulation in bars 1 through 18

Bar 4: The B♭maj7 has a split function in the main key as the VI chord, and begins the modulation to B♭ Major acting as the I chord.

Bar 6: The D7 is the minor 3rd substitution for the V chord in B♭ Major (F7). It mimics a IV → V in B♭ Major, dropping down a half step from E♭ to D and then begins a new modulation to G Major.

Bar 11: The Gmaj7 resolves the modulation to G Major and begins a root cycle where the root of each chord ascends by an interval of a minor 2nd.

Bar 13: The A7 ends the root cycle and splits its function as the V chord in D Minor, returning the song to the main key.

Bar 17: Dmaj7 functions as the tonic interchange for Dm7, resolving the progression in D Minor to the Imaj7 instead of the Im7. This loosely resembles the effect of a Tierce de Picardie (see page 28).

Example 209: Bars 39-50 of "Circle."

Bar 43: A modulation to B♭ Major is entered using the V chord (F7). The Gm7 in the previous bar also has a function in B♭ Major as the VI chord, providing a relationship between the two chords.

Bar 47: The E♭maj7 ends the modulation to B♭ Major functioning as the IV chord. It is also the common tritone substitution for the V chord (A7) in D Minor, with its species altered to a maj7th. This is reinforced as the E♭maj7 actually moves a tritone away to the A7 (E♭ root to A root).

Miles concentrates almost exclusively on the effect of single notes against the chords. He, of course, employs chord tones, upper partials, and alterations to accomplish this. The scale substitutions are enabling Miles to use the notes he wants over the chords, and not to create the more "outside" feel his scale substitutions may have created in other solos.

PART IV | THE SOLOS

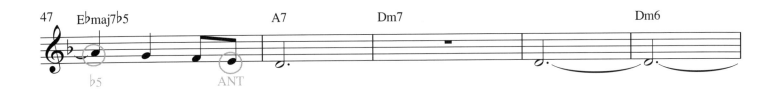

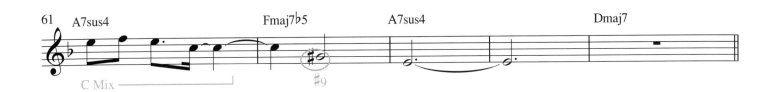

PETITS MACHINS
From the recording *Filles de Kilimanjaro* (Miles Davis)

By Miles Davis and Gil Evans

PETITS MACHINS

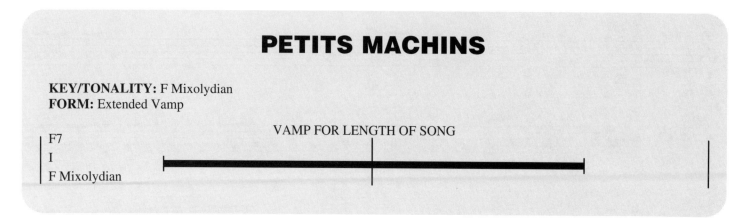

KEY/TONALITY: F Mixolydian
FORM: Extended Vamp

F7
I
F Mixolydian

VAMP FOR LENGTH OF SONG

"Petits Machins" is written in F Mixolydian with emphasis on the I chord, F7 (see "It's About That Time," page 151, for explanation of usage). Miles based his entire solo on or against the F7 chord. His solo alternates between the F Mixolydian scale and the F Natural Minor scale. The F Natural Minor scale offers the blue note ♭3rd/♯9th (A♭), and the ♭13th (D♭) against the F7, providing some added color to the solo. Miles plays the F Mixolydian and F Natural Minor scales against each other (notably the A♮ and A♭) as he sets up one main motif that runs through his solo. Miles used other scale substitutions as well, for "Petits Machins," often blending two scales in the middle of a phrase.

THE MUSIC OF MILES DAVIS

SPANISH KEY
From the recording *Bitches Brew* (Miles Davis)

By Miles Davis

PART IV | THE SOLOS

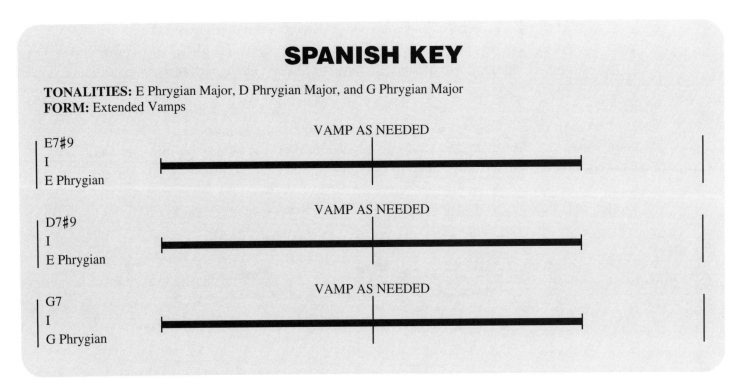

"SPANISH KEY"

"Spanish Key" was written using the phrygian major technique, which gives a song a flamenco or "Spanish" sound, as the title suggests. This technique uses a phrygian major scale (♭2, ♭6, ♭7) for the chords, while the soloist uses a phrygian scale (♭2, ♭3, ♭6, ♭7). See page 29 for further information on phrygian major.

The melody that Miles created for "Spanish Key" in bars 1-19 uses an E Mixolydian scale with the ♯9th (G♮) added. This ties "Spanish Key" to the writing style of the other songs Miles wrote during this time ("Petit Machin," "It's About That Time," and "Miles Runs the Voodoo Down," for example).

Example 210: "Spanish Key" (head only).

311

It is not until the solo section that the song switches to phrygian major. Miles uses three different sections in the solos for "Spanish Key," each using phrygian major: E Phrygian Major, D Phrygian Major, and G Phrygian Major. The length of each section in terms of bar numbers is at the discretion of the players. So, there are no pre-set bar lengths for each scale. Miles begins his solo in bar 20. The band continues playing off the E7#9 chord that was used in E Mixolydian and now is usable as part of E Phrygian Major. Miles uses the E Phrygian scale exclusively during the E Phrygian Major section, with a chromatic auxilary tone added in bars 24 and 25.

Example 211: Bars 20-29 of Miles' solo for "Spanish Key."

In bar 30, the song switches to D Phrygian Major, where the band plays out of the D Phrygian Major scale (D E♭ F♯ G A B♭ C) and Miles solos using the D Phrygian scale (D E♭ F G A B♭ C).

Example 212: Bars 30-47 of Miles' solo for "Spanish Key."

SELECTED DISCOGRAPHY with recording dates

♪	Charlie Parker	*The Immortal Charlie Parker, Volume 2* (9/44, 11/45, 5/47, 8/47)
	Charlie Parker	*Charlie Parker Memorial, Volume 1* (5/47, 12/47, 9/48)
♪	Charlie Parker	*Charlie Parker Memorial, Volume 2* (11/45, 8/47, 5/48, 9/48)
	Charlie Parker	*The Genius of Charlie Parker* (11/45, 12/45, 5/47, 12/47, 9/48)
	Charlie Parker	*Swedish Schnapps* (5/49, 1/51, 8/51)
♪	Miles Davis	*Birth of the Cool* (1/49, 4/49, 3/50)
	Miles Davis	*Miles Davis and Horns* (1/51, 2/53)
	Sonny Rollins	*Sonny Rollins with the Modern Jazz Quartet* (1/51, 12/51, 10/53)
	Miles Davis	*Conception* (6/49, 10/51)
♪	Miles Davis	*Dig* (10/51)
	Miles Davis	*Miles Davis, Volume 1* (5/52)
	Miles Davis	*Miles Davis, Volume 2* (4/53)
♪	Miles Davis	*Collector's Items* (1/53, 3/56)
♪	Miles Davis	*Blue Haze* (3/54)
♪	Miles Davis All Stars	*Walkin'* (4/54)
	Miles Davis	*Bags' Groove* (6/54)
	Miles Davis	*Green Haze* (6/55)
♪	Miles Davis	*Miles Davis and the Modern Jazz Giants* (12/54, 10/56)
♪	Miles Davis	*Workin'* (5/56, 10/56)
	Miles Davis	*Musings of Miles* (6/55)
	Miles Davis	*Blue Moods* (7/55)
	Miles Davis	*Miles Davis and Milt Jackson Quintet/Sextet* (8/55)
	Miles Davis	*Miles* (11/55)
	Miles Davis	*Circle in the Round* (10/55, 5/58. 3/61, 12/67)

♪ Indicates the albums with songs that are transcribed in this book.

DISCOGRAPHY

Miles Davis	*Steamin'* (5/56, 10/56)
Miles Davis	*Relaxin'* (5/56, 10/56)
Miles Davis	*Round About Midnight* (10/55, 6-9/56)
Miles Davis	*Music for Brass* (10/56)
♪ Miles Davis	*Cookin'* (10/56)
Various Artists	*The Birth of the Third Stream* (10/56, 4/57, 6/57)
♪ Miles Davis	*Miles Ahead* (5/57)
Julian "Cannonball" Adderly	*Somethin' Else* (3/58)
♪ Miles Davis	*Milestones* (2/58, 4/58)
Miles Davis	*1958 Miles* (5/58, 7/58)
Miles Davis and John Coltrane	*Miles & Coltrane* (10/55, 7/58)
Michel Legrand	*Legrand Jazz* (6/58)
♪ Cannonball Adderly	*Portrait of Cannonball* (7/1/58)
Miles Davis	*Miles & Monk at Newport* (7/58)
Miles Davis	*Porgy and Bess* (7-8/58)
♪ Miles Davis	*Kind of Blue* (3-4/59)
Miles Davis	*Sketches of Spain* (11/59, 3/60)
♪ Miles Davis	*Someday My Prince Will Come* (3/61)
Miles Davis	*In Person: Friday and Saturday Nights at the Blackhawk* (4/61)
♪ Miles Davis	*At Carnegie Hall* (5/61)
Miles Davis	*Quiet Nights* (7/62, 8/62, 11/62, 4/63, 10/63)
♪ Miles Davis	*Seven Steps to Heaven* (4-5/63)
♪ Miles Davis	*The Complete Concert 1964 (My Funny Valentine + Four & More)* (2/64)
♪ Miles Davis	*E.S.P.* (1/65)
♪ Bill Evans	*The Secret Sessions* (3/66-1/26/75, 8/23/62-5/24/67)

	Miles Davis	*Sorcerer* (5/67)
	Miles Davis	*The Complete Live at the Plugged Nickel 1965* (12/65)
♪	Miles Davis	*Miles Smiles* (10/66)
	Miles Davis	*Nefertiti* (6-7/67)
♪	Miles Davis	*Miles in the Sky* (1/68, 4-5/68)
♪	Miles Davis	*Filles de Kilimanjaro* (6/68, 9/68)
♪	Bill Evans	*Bill Evans at the Montreux Jazz Festival* (6/15/68)
♪	Miles Davis	*In a Silent Way* (2/69)
♪	Miles Davis	*Bitches Brew* (8/69)
♪	Bill Evans	*You're Gonna Hear from Me* (11/24/69)
	Miles Davis	*Live-Evil* (6/70)
	Miles Davis	*A Tribute to Jack Johnson* (4/70)
	Miles Davis	*On the Corner* (6/72)
	Miles Davis	*Agharta* (2/75)
	Miles Davis	*Pangea* (2/75)
♪	Bill Evans	*Turn out the Stars* (8/2/80)
	Miles Davis	*The Man with the Horn* (1-4/81)
	Miles Davis	*We Want Miles* (6/81)
	Miles Davis	*Star People* (8/11/62, 1-2/83)
	Miles Davis	*Decoy* (7/83, 9-10/83)
	Miles Davis	*You're under Arrest* (5/85)
	Miles Davis	*Tutu* (1986)
	Miles Davis	*Amandla* (8/89)
	Miles Davis	*Aura* (9/89, 1/31/85-2/4/85)
	Miles Davis and Quincy Jones	*Live at Montreux* (7/91)

The Best Selling Jazz Book of All Time Is Now Legal!

The Real Books are the most popular jazz books of all time. Since the 1970s, musicians have trusted these volumes to get them through every gig, night after night. The problem is that the books were illegally produced and distributed, without any regard to copyright law, or royalties paid to the composers who created these musical masterpieces.

Hal Leonard is very proud to present the first legitimate and legal editions of these books ever produced. You won't even notice the difference, other than all the notorious errors being fixed: the covers and typeface look the same, the song lists are nearly identical, and the price for our edition is even cheaper than the originals!

Every conscientious musician will appreciate that these books are now produced accurately and ethically, benefitting the songwriters that we owe for some of the greatest tunes of all time!

Volume 1 includes: Autumn Leaves • Black Orpheus • Bluesette • Body and Soul • Don't Get Around Much Anymore • Falling in Love with Love • Footprints • Giant Steps • Have You Met Miss Jones? • Lullaby of Birdland • Misty • Satin Doll • Stella by Starlight • and hundreds more!

Volume 2 includes: Avalon • Basin Street Blues • Birdland • Come Rain or Come Shine • Fever • Fly Me to the Moon • Georgia on My Mind • It Might As Well Be Spring • Moonglow • The Nearness of You • On the Sunny Side of the Street • Route 66 • Sentimental Journey • Smoke Gets in Your Eyes • Tangerine • Yardbird Suite • and more!

Volume 1
00240221 C Edition $25.00
00240224 B♭ Edition $25.00
00240225 E♭ Edition $25.00

Volume 2
00240222 C Edition $25.00

For More Information, See Your Local Music Dealer, Or Write To:

HAL•LEONARD® CORPORATION
7777 W. Bluemound Rd. P.O. Box 13819 Milwaukee, WI 53213

Complete song lists online at www.halleonard.com

Prices and availability subject to change without notice.

Presenting the Hal Leonard JAZZ PLAY ALONG SERIES

DUKE ELLINGTON Vol. 1 00841644
Caravan • Don't Get Around Much Anymore • In a Mellow Tone • In a Sentimental Mood • It Don't Mean a Thing (If It Ain't Got That Swing) • Perdido • Prelude to a Kiss • Satin Doll • Sophisticated Lady • Take the "A" Train.

MILES DAVIS Vol. 2 00841645
All Blues • Blue in Green • Four • Half Nelson • Milestones • Nardis • Seven Steps to Heaven • So What • Solar • Tune Up.

THE BLUES Vol. 3 00841646
Billie's Bounce • Birk's Works • Blues for Alice • Blues in the Closet • C-Jam Blues • Freddie Freeloader • Mr. P.C. • Now's the Time • Tenor Madness • Things Ain't What They Used to Be.

JAZZ BALLADS Vol. 4 00841691
Body and Soul • But Beautiful • Here's That Rainy Day • Misty • My Foolish Heart • My Funny Valentine • My One and Only Love • My Romance • The Nearness of You.

BEST OF BEBOP Vol. 5 00841689
Anthropology • Donna Lee • Doxy • Epistrophy • Lady Bird • Oleo • Ornithology • Scrapple from the Apple • Woodyn' You • Yardbird Suite.

JAZZ CLASSICS WITH EASY CHANGES Vol. 6 00841690
Blue Train • Comin' Home Baby • Footprints • Impressions • Killer Joe • Moanin' • Sidewinder • St. Thomas • Stolen Moments • Well You Needn't.

ESSENTIAL JAZZ STANDARDS Vol. 7 00843000
Autumn Leaves • Cotton Tail • Easy Living • I Remember You • If I Should Lose You • Lullaby of Birdland • Out of Nowhere • Stella by Starlight • There Will Never Be Another You • When Sunny Gets Blue.

ANTONIO CARLOS JOBIM AND THE ART OF THE BOSSA NOVA Vol. 8 00843001
The Girl from Ipanema • How Insensitive • Meditation • Once I Loved • One Note Samba • Quiet Nights of Quiet Stars • Slightly Out of Tune • So Danco Samba • Triste • Wave.

DIZZY GILLESPIE Vol. 9 00843002
Birk's Works • Con Alma • Groovin' High • Manteca • A Night in Tunisia • Salt Peanuts • Shawnuff • Things to Come • Tour De Force • Woodyn' You.

DISNEY CLASSICS Vol. 10 00843003
Alice in Wonderland • Beauty and the Beast • Cruella De Vil • Heigh-Ho • Some Day My Prince Will Come • When You Wish upon a Star • Whistle While You Work • Who's Afraid of the Big Bad Wolf • You've Got a Friend in Me • Zip-a-Dee-Doo-Dah.

RODGERS AND HART FAVORITES Vol. 11 00843004
Bewitched • The Blue Room • Dancing on the Ceiling • Have You Met Miss Jones? • I Could Write a Book • The Lady Is a Tramp • Little Girl Blue • My Romance • There's a Small Hotel • You Are Too Beautiful.

ESSENTIAL JAZZ CLASSICS Vol. 12 00843005
Airegin • Ceora • The Frim Fram Sauce • Israel • Milestones • Nefertiti • Red Clay • Satin Doll • Song for My Father • Take Five.

JOHN COLTRANE Vol. 13 00843006
Blue Train • Countdown • Cousin Mary • Equinox • Giant Steps • Impressions • Lazy Bird • Mr. P.C. • Moment's Notice • Naima.

IRVING BERLIN Vol. 14 00843007
Be Careful, It's My Heart • Blue Skies • Change Partners • Cheek to Cheek • I've Got My Love to Keep Me Warm • Steppin' Out with My Baby • They Say It's Wonderful • What'll I Do?

RODGERS & HAMMERSTEIN Vol. 15 00843008
Bali Ha'i • Do I Love You Because You're Beautiful? • Hello Young Lovers • I Have Dreamed • It Might as Well Be Spring • Love, Look Away • My Favorite Things • The Surrey with the Fringe on Top • The Sweetest Sounds • Younger Than Springtime.

COLE PORTER Vol. 16 00843009
All of You • At Long Last • Easy to Love • Ev'ry Time We Say Goodbye • I Concentrate on You • I've Got You Under My Skin • In the Still of the Night • It's All Right with Me • It's De-Lovely • You'd Be So Nice to Come Home To.

COUNT BASIE Vol. 17 00843010
All of Me • April in Paris • Blues in Hoss Flat • Cute • Jumpin' at the Woodside • Li'l Darlin' • Moten Swing • One O'Clock Jump • Shiny Stockings • Until I Met You.

HAROLD ARLEN Vol. 18 00843011
Ac-cent-tchu-ate the Positive • Between the Devil and the Deep Blue Sea • Come Rain or Come Shine • If I Only Had a Brain • It's Only a Paper Moon • I've Got the World on a String • My Shining Hour • Over the Rainbow • Stormy Weather • That Old Black Magic.

COOL JAZZ Vol. 19 00843012
Bernie's Tune • Boplicity • Budo • Conception • Django • Five Brothers • Line for Lyons • Walkin' Shoes • Waltz for Debby • Whisper Not.

RODGERS AND HART CLASSICS Vol. 21 00843014
Falling in Love with Love • Isn't it Romantic? • Manhattan • Mountain Greenery • My Funny Valentine • My Heart Stood Still • This Can't Be Love • Thou Swell • Where or When • You Took Advantage of Me.

WAYNE SHORTER Vol. 22 00843015
Children of the Night • ESP • Footprints • Juju • Mahjong • Nefertiti • Nightdreamer • Speak No Evil • Witch Hunt • Yes and No.

LATIN JAZZ Vol. 23 00843016
Agua De Beber • Chega De Saudade • The Gift! • Invitation • Manha De Carnaval • Mas Que Nada • Ran Kan Kan • So Nice • Sweet Happy Life • Watch What Happens.

EARLY JAZZ STANDARDS Vol. 24 00843017
After You've Gone • Avalon • Indian Summer • Indiana (Back Home Again in Indiana) • Ja-Da • Limehouse Blues • Paper Doll • Poor Butterfly • Rose Room • St. Louis Blues.

CHRISTMAS JAZZ Vol. 25 00843018
The Christmas Song (Chestnuts Roasting on an Open Fire) • The Christmas Waltz • Frosty the Snow Man • Home for the Holidays • I Heard the Bells on Christmas Day • I'll Be Home for Christmas • Let It Snow! Let It Snow! Let It Snow! • Rudolph the Red-Nosed Reindeer • Silver Bells • Snowfall.

CHARLIE PARKER Vol. 26 00843019
Au Privave • Billie's Bounce • Confirmation • Donna Lee • Moose the Mooche • My Little Suede Shoes • Now's the Time • Ornithology • Scrapple from the Apple • Yardbird Suite.

GREAT JAZZ STANDARDS Vol. 27 00843020
Fly Me to the Moon • Girl Talk • How High the Moon • I Can't Get Started with You • It Could Happen to You • Lover • Softly As in a Morning Sunrise • Speak Low • Tangerine • Willow Weep for Me.

BIG BAND ERA Vol. 28 00843021
Air Mail Special • Christopher Columbus • Four Brothers • In the Mood • Intermission Riff • Jersey Bounce • Opus One • Stompin' at the Savoy • A String of Pearls • Tuxedo Junction.

LENNON AND MCCARTNEY Vol. 29 00843022
And I Love Her • Blackbird • Come Together • Eleanor Rigby • The Fool on the Hill • Here, There and Everywhere • Lady Madonna • Let It Be • Ticket to Ride • Yesterday.

BLUES BEST Vol. 30 00843023
Basin Street Blues • Bloomdido • D Natural Blues • Everyday I Have the Blues Again • Happy Go Lucky Local • K.C. Blues • Sonnymoon for Two • The Swingin' Shepherd Blues • Take the Coltrane • Turnaround.

JAZZ IN THREE Vol. 31 00843024
Bluesette • Gravy Waltz • Jitterbug Waltz • Moon River • Oh, What a Beautiful Mornin' • Tenderly • Tennessee Waltz • West Coast Blues • What the World Needs Now Is Love • Wives and Lovers.

BEST OF SWING Vol. 32 00843025
Alright, Okay, You Win • Cherokee • I'll Be Seeing You • I've Heard That Song Before • Java Jive • Jump, Jive An' Wail • On the Sunny Side of the Street • Route 66 • Sentimental Journey • What's New?

SONNY ROLLINS Vol. 33 00843029
Airegin • Alfie's Theme • Biji • Doxy • Here's to the People • Oleo • St. Thomas • Sonnymoon for Two.

ALL TIME STANDARDS Vol. 34 00843030
Autumn in New York • Bye Bye Blackbird • Call Me Irresponsible • Georgia on My Miind • Honeysuckle Rose • I'll Remember April • Stardust • There Is No Greater Love • The Very Thought of You • Broadway.

BLUESY JAZZ Vol. 35 00843031
Angel Eyes • Bags' Groove • Bessie's Blues • Chitlins Con Carne • Good Morning Heartache • High Fly • Mercy, Mercy, Mercy • Night Train • Sugar • Sweet Georgia Bright.

HORACE SILVER Vol. 36 00843032
Doodlin' • The Jody Grind • Nica's Dream • Peace • The Preacher • Senor Blues • Sister Sadie • Song for My Father • Strollin'.

BILL EVANS Vol. 37 00843033
Funkallero • My Bells • One for Helen • The Opener • Orbit • Show-Type Tune • 34 Skidoo • Time Remembered • Turn Out the Stars • Waltz for Debby.

YULETIDE JAZZ Vol. 38 00843034
Blue Christmas • Christmas Time Is Here • Feliz Navidad • Happy Holiday • Here Comes Santa Claus • A Marshmallow World • Merry Christmas, Darling • The Most Wonderful Time of the Year • My Favorite Things • Santa Claus Is Comin' to Town.

ALL THE THINGS YOU ARE & MORE JEROME KERN SONGS Vol. 39 00843035
All the Things You Are • Can't Help Lovin' Dat Man • Dearly Beloved • A Fine Romance • The Folks Who Live on the Hill • Long Ago (And Far Away) • Pick Yourself Up • The Song Is You • The Way You Look Tonight • Yesterday.

BOSSA NOVA Vol. 40 00843036
Black Orpheus • Call Me • Dindi • Little Boat • A Man and a Woman • Only Trust Your Heart • The Shadow of Your Smile • Song of the Jet (Samba do Aviao) • Watch What Happens • Wave.

CLASSIC DUKE ELLINGTON Vol. 41 00843037
C-Jam Blues • Come Sunday • Cotton Tail • Do Nothin' Till You Hear from Me • I Got It Bad and That Ain't Good • I Let a Song Go Out of My Heart • I'm Beginning to See the Light • I'm Just a Lucky So and So • Mood Indigo • Solitude.

GERRY MULLIGAN FAVORITES Vol. 42 00843038
Bark for Barksdale • Dragonfly • Elevation • Idol Gossip • Jeru • The Lonely Night (Night Lights) • Noblesse • Rock Salt a/k/a Rocker • Theme for Jobim • Wallflower.

GERRY MULLIGAN CLASSICS Vol. 43 00843039
Apple Core • A Ballad • Festive Minor • Five Brothers • Line for Lyons • Nights at the Turntable • North Atlantic Run • Song for Strayhorn • Sun on the Stairs • Walkin' Shoes.

BOOK/CD PACKAGES
ONLY $14.95 EACH!

The Hal Leonard JAZZ PLAY ALONG SERIES is the ultimate learning tool for all jazz musicians. With musician-friendly lead sheets, melody cues and other split track choices on the included CD, this first-of-its-kind package makes learning to play jazz easier and more fun than ever before.

Prices, contents and availability subject to change without notice.

FOR MORE INFORMATION,
SEE YOUR LOCAL MUSIC DEALER,
OR WRITE TO:

HAL•LEONARD
CORPORATION
7777 W. BLUEMOUND RD. P.O. BOX 13819
MILWAUKEE, WISCONSIN 53213

Visit Hal Leonard online at
www.halleonard.com

0804

Jazz Improvisation Workshop

An exciting new improvisation method designed for all levels of players – from the absolute beginner to the experienced performer. Instructional volumes can be used individually or in a group/classroom environment. Play-along song collections feature musical variety, top-notch rhythm section accompaniment, great tunes, and performance of each head as well as choruses for improvisation. Each book includes a play-along CD.

Patterns For Beginning Improvisation
For All Instruments • by Frank Mantooth

From The Beginning
This beginning improvisation method is designed for students who are beginners in jazz – no prior jazz experience is necessary to use this book. The patterns begin simply and gradually increase in difficulty.
00841100 C Inst
00841101 Bb Inst
00841102 Eb Inst
00841103 Bass Clef

Movin' On To The Blues
This method for blues improvisation is designed for students with minimal jazz experience. Simple patterns are presented with easy, but frequently encountered progressions.
00841104 C Inst
00841105 Bb Inst
00841106 Eb Inst
00841107 Bass Clef

Jazz Standards Play-Along Collections

Jazz Classic Standards
15 songs, including: All Of Me • Don't Get Around Much Anymore • Milestones • My Funny Valentine • Opus One • When I Fall In Love • and more.
00841120 C Inst
00841121 Bb Inst
00841122 Eb Inst
00841123 Bass Clef

Jazz Favorites
15 songs, including: Bewitched • Bye Bye Blackbird • How High The Moon • Now's The Time • Speak Low • and more.
00841124 C Inst
00841125 Bb Inst
00841126 Eb Inst
00841127 Bass Clef

Essential Jazz Standards
15 songs, including: The Girl From Ipanema • Groovin' High • Have You Met Miss Jones? • It Could Happen To You • It Might As Well Be Spring • Long Ago And Far Away • A Night In Tunisia • Stella By Starlight • and more.
00841128 C Inst
00841129 Bb Inst
00841130 Eb Inst
00841131 Bass Clef

Jazz Gems
15 songs, including: All The Things You Are • Bluesette • Epistrophy • How Insensitive • My Funny Valentine • My Romance • Satin Doll • Summer Samba (So Nice) • Tangerine • and more.
00841132 C Inst
00841133 Bb Inst
00841134 Eb Inst
00841135 Bass Clef

For More Information, See Your Local Music Dealer, Or Write To:

7777 W. Bluemound Rd. P.O. Box 13819 Milwaukee, WI 53213

Visit Hal Leonard on the internet at http://www.halleonard.com
Prices, contents, and availability subject to change without notice. Some products may not be available outside the U.S.A.

ARTIST TRANSCRIPTIONS

Artist Transcriptions are authentic, note-for-note transcriptions of the hottest artists in jazz, pop, and rock today. These outstanding, accurate arrangements are in an easy-to-read format which includes all essential lines. Artist Transcriptions can be used to perform, sequence or reference.

GUITAR & BASS

The Guitar Style of George Benson
00660113 .... $14.95

The Guitar Book of Pierre Bensusan
00699072 .... $19.95

Ron Carter – Acoustic Bass
00672331 .... $16.95

Stanley Clarke Collection
00672307 .... $19.95

Al Di Meola – Cielo E Terra
00604041 .... $14.95

Al Di Meola – Friday Night in San Francisco
00660115 .... $14.95

Al Di Meola – Music, Words, Pictures
00604043 .... $14.95

Kevin Eubanks Guitar Collection
00672319 .... $19.95

The Jazz Style of Tal Farlow
00673245 .... $19.95

Bela Fleck and the Flecktones
00672359 Melody/Lyrics/Chords $18.95

David Friesen – Years Through Time
00673253 .... $14.95

Best of Frank Gambale
00672336 .... $22.95

Jim Hall – Jazz Guitar Environments
00699389 Book/CD $19.95

Jim Hall – Exploring Jazz Guitar
00699306 .... $17.95

Allan Holdsworth – Reaching for the Uncommon Chord
00604049 .... $14.95

Leo Kottke – Eight Songs
00699215 .... $14.95

Wes Montgomery – Guitar Transcriptions
00675536 .... $17.95

Joe Pass Collection
00672353 .... $18.95

John Patitucci
00673216 .... $14.95

Django Reinhardt Anthology
00027083 .... $14.95

The Genius of Django Reinhardt
00026711 .... $10.95

Django Reinhardt – A Treasury of Songs
00026715 .... $12.95

Johnny Smith Guitar Solos
00672374 .... $16.95

Mike Stern Guitar Book
00673224 .... $16.95

Mark Whitfield
00672320 .... $19.95

Jack Wilkins – Windows
00673249 .... $14.95

Gary Willis Collection
00672337 .... $19.95

SAXOPHONE

Julian "Cannonball" Adderly Collection
00673244 .... $19.95

Michael Brecker
00673237 .... $19.95

Michael Brecker Collection
00672429 .... $19.95

The Brecker Brothers... And All Their Jazz
00672351 .... $19.95

Best of the Brecker Brothers
00672447 .... $19.95

Benny Carter Plays Standards
00672315 .... $22.95

Benny Carter Collection
00672314 .... $22.95

James Carter Collection
00672394 .... $19.95

John Coltrane – Giant Steps
00672349 .... $19.95

John Coltrane – A Love Supreme
00672494 .... $12.95

John Coltrane Plays "Coltrane Changes"
00672493 .... $19.95

Coltrane Plays Standards
00672453 .... $19.95

John Coltrane Solos
00673233 .... $22.95

Paul Desmond Collection
00672328 .... $19.95

Paul Desmond – Standard Time
00672454 .... $19.95

Stan Getz
00699375 .... $18.95

Stan Getz – Bossa Novas
00672377 .... $19.95

Stan Getz – Standards
00672375 .... $17.95

The Coleman Hawkins Collection
00672523 .... $19.95

Joe Henderson – Selections from "Lush Life" & "So Near So Far"
00672252 .... $19.95

Best of Joe Henderson
00672330 .... $22.95

Best of Kenny G
00673239 .... $19.95

Kenny G – Breathless
00673229 .... $19.95

Kenny G – Classics in the Key of G
00672462 .... $19.95

Kenny G – Faith: A Holiday Album
00672485 .... $14.95

Kenny G – The Moment
00672373 .... $19.95

Kenny G – Paradise
00672516 .... $14.95

Joe Lovano Collection
00672326 .... $19.95

James Moody Collection – Sax and Flute
00672372 .... $19.95

The Frank Morgan Collection
00672416 .... $19.95

The Art Pepper Collection
00672301 .... $19.95

Sonny Rollins Collection
00672444 .... $19.95

David Sanborn Collection
00675000 .... $16.95

The Lew Tabackin Collection
00672455 .... $19.95

Stanley Turrentine Collection
00672334 .... $19.95

Ernie Watts Saxophone Collection
00673256 .... $18.95

PIANO & KEYBOARD

Monty Alexander Collection
00672338 .... $19.95

Monty Alexander Plays Standards
00672487 .... $19.95

Kenny Barron Collection
00672318 .... $22.95

The Count Basie Collection
00672520 .... $19.95

Warren Bernhardt Collection
00672364 .... $19.95

Cyrus Chesnut Collection
00672439 .... $19.95

Billy Childs Collection
00673242 .... $19.95

Chick Corea – Elektric Band
00603126 .... $15.95

Chick Corea – Paint the World
00672300 .... $12.95

Bill Evans Collection
00672365 .... $19.95

Bill Evans – Piano Interpretations
00672425 .... $19.95

The Bill Evans Trio
00672510 Volume 1: 1959-1961 ...... $24.95
00672511 Volume 2: 1962-1965 ...... $24.95
00672512 Volume 3: 1968-1974 ...... $24.95
00672513 Volume 4: 1979-1980 ...... $24.95

The Benny Goodman Collection
00672492 .... $16.95

Benny Green Collection
00672329 .... $19.95

Vince Guaraldi Jazz Transcriptions
00672486 .... $19.95

Herbie Hancock Collection
00672419 .... $19.95

Gene Harris Collection
00672446 .... $19.95

Hampton Hawes
00672438 .... $19.95

Ahmad Jamal Collection
00672322 .... $22.95

Brad Mehldau Collection
00672476 .... $19.95

Thelonious Monk Plays Jazz Standards – Volume 1
00672390 .... $19.95

Thelonious Monk Plays Jazz Standards – Volume 2
00672391 .... $19.95

Thelonious Monk – Intermediate Piano Solos
00672392 .... $14.95

Jelly Roll Morton – The Piano Rolls
00672433 .... $12.95

Michel Petrucciani
00673226 .... $17.95

Bud Powell Classics
00672371 .... $19.95

Bud Powell Collection
00672376 .... $19.95

André Previn Collection
00672437 .... $19.95

Gonzalo Rubalcaba Collection
00672507 .... $19.95

Horace Silver Collection
00672303 .... $19.95

Art Tatum Collection
00672316 .... $22.95

Art Tatum Solo Book
00672355 .... $19.95

Billy Taylor Collection
00672357 .... $24.95

McCoy Tyner
00673215 .... $16.95

Cedar Walton Collection
00672321 .... $19.95

The Teddy Wilson Collection
00672434 .... $19.95

CLARINET

Buddy De Franco Collection
00672423 .... $19.95

TROMBONE

J.J. Johnson Collection
00672332 .... $19.95

TRUMPET

The Chet Baker Collection
00672435 .... $19.95

Randy Brecker
00673234 .... $17.95

The Brecker Brothers...And All Their Jazz
00672351 .... $19.95

Best of the Brecker Brothers
00672447 .... $19.95

Miles Davis – Originals Volume 1
00672448 .... $19.95

Miles Davis – Originals Volume 2
00672451 .... $19.95

Miles Davis – Standards Vol. 1
00672450 .... $19.95

Miles Davis – Standards Vol. 2
00672449 .... $19.95

The Dizzy Gillespie Collection
00672479 .... $19.95

Freddie Hubbard
00673214 .... $14.95

Tom Harrell Jazz Trumpet
00672382 .... $19.95

The Chuck Mangione Collection
00672506 .... $19.95

FLUTE

Eric Dolphy Collection
00672379 .... $19.95

James Newton – Improvising Flute
00660108 .... $14.95

The Lew Tabackin Collection
00672455 .... $19.95

FOR MORE INFORMATION, SEE YOUR LOCAL MUSIC DEALER, OR WRITE TO:

HAL•LEONARD CORPORATION
7777 W. BLUEMOUND RD. P.O. BOX 13819 MILWAUKEE, WI 53213

Prices and availability subject to change without notice.
Some products may not be available outside the U.S.A.

Visit our web site for a complete listing of our titles with songlists.
www.halleonard.com

Secondary dominant chords occur in every genre of music and it's important to understand their function in harmony. Most songs would be pretty bland if they consisted only of diatonic chords.

Now remember that the primary dominant, [the V7 chord,](#) which resolves down a fifth to the I chord, is an important building block of music. Well, the other diatonic chords each have their own "secondary" dominant chord.

Here are the secondary dominants in C major:

The II-7 chord (D-7) has the secondary dominant of A7. This is called the V7 of II or V7/II and occurs in that classic progression:
Cmaj7 A7 D-7 G7.

The secondary dominant of the III-7 (E-7) is a B7 and is labeled V7/III.

The secondary dominant of IVmaj7 (Fmaj7) is a C7 and is labeled V7/IV.

Yes, even the primary dominant (G7) has it's own secondary dominant which is D7. The V7/V occurs extremely often, especially in classical music.

The secondary dominant of VI-7 (A-7) is an E7 and labeled V7/VI.

However, there is rarely a V7/VII chord so don't worry about that one.

Secondary dominants will often be used in the middle of a progression or at the end to transition to a new section. Secondary dominants are also used to modulate to a new key by becoming the new primary dominant of the new key.

Also, secondary dominants, as well as primary dominants, don't always have to resolve down a fifth. Often dominant chords will "deceptively" resolve to a different chord. Deceptive resolutions sound great because they keep the energy of the progression building.

Here's an example of secondary dominants and deceptive resolutions in the begining chord progression of the standard, On the Sunny Side of the Street:

Cmaj7 (Imaj7), E7 (V7/VI), which then deceptively resolves to Fmaj7 (IVmaj7), G7 (V7), which also deceptively resolves to A-7 (VI-7), D7 (V7/V), D-7 (II-7), G7 (V7), Cmaj7 (Imaj7).